xaminations
o January 2012

AS Music Study Guide

OCR

Veronica Jamset, Susan Wynne Roberts
and Huw Ellis-Williams

Edited by
Paul Terry

R·

Rhinegold Education

239–241 Shaftesbury Avenue
London WC2H 8TF
Telephone: 020 7333 1720
Fax: 020 7333 1765

www.rhinegold.co.uk

Rhinegold Music Study Guides
(series editor: Paul Terry)

GCSE, AS and A2 Music Study Guides (AQA, Edexcel and OCR)
GCSE, AS and A2 Music Listening Tests (AQA, Edexcel and OCR)
GCSE Music Study Guide (WJEC)
AS/A2 Music Technology Study Guide (Edexcel)
AS and A2 Music Technology Listening Tests (Edexcel)
Lifelines Revision Guides for GCSE, AS and A2 Music (AQA and Edexcel)
Lifelines Revision Guide for GCSE Music (OCR)
Lifelines Revision Guides for AS and A2 Music Technology (Edexcel)
AS and A2 Music Harmony Workbooks
GCSE Music Composition Workbook
GCSE Music Literacy Workbook

Also available from Rhinegold Education

Key Stage 3 Elements
Key Stage 3 Listening Tests: Book 1 and Book 2
Baroque Music in Focus, Romanticism in Focus, Modernism in Focus
Batman in Focus, *Goldfinger* in Focus, Madonna in Focus, *Who's Next* in Focus
Film Music in Focus, Musicals in Focus

Rhinegold Publishing also publishes Classical Music, Classroom Music, Early Music Today, Music Teacher, Opera Now, Piano, Teaching Drama, The Singer, British and International Music Yearbook, British Performing Arts Yearbook, Rhinegold Guide to Music Education, Rhinegold Dictionary of Music in Sound.

Other Rhinegold Study Guides

Rhinegold publishes resources for candidates studying Classical Civilisation, Drama and Theatre Studies, Performance Studies and Religious Studies.

First published 2008 in Great Britain by
Rhinegold Publishing Limited
239–241 Shaftesbury Avenue
London WC2H 8TF
Telephone: 020 7333 1720
Fax: 020 7333 1765
www.rhinegold.co.uk

You should always check the current requirements of the examination, since these may change. Copies of the OCR Specification can be downloaded from the OCR website at http://www.ocr.org.uk/ or may be purchased from OCR Publications, PO Box 5050, Annersley, Nottingham NG15 0DL
Telephone 0870 870 6622   Email: publications@ocr.org.uk

OCR AS Music Study Guide (June 2009–January 2012)
British Library Cataloguing in Publication Data.
A catalogue record for this book is available from the British Library.
ISBN 978-1-906178-26-0
Printed in Great Britain by Headley Brothers Ltd

Contents

(*) The first three jazz recordings in this list are set for examinations from June 2009 until January 2011 while the remaining three are set for examinations from June 2011 onwards.

The details of the specification are believed to be correct at the time of going to press, but you and your teachers should always check current requirements for the examination with OCR since these may change. The music specification is available at www.ocr.org.uk

The authors

Veronica Jamset taught music to young people aged between four and 18 years, in primary and secondary schools, selective and non-selective, in both the state and private sectors in the West Midlands, before taking up her first post in Higher Education as a teacher trainer. She worked in two colleges in Birmingham and then moved to St Mary's College at Strawberry Hill in Twickenham, where she became principal lecturer in music and director of in-service and continuing education. Veronica also has considerable experience in adult education. She has been an examiner at various levels since 1990 and, until 2000, was chief examiner for OCR's AS and A-level music syllabuses. She was a member of the team that drafted OCR's current AS/A2 music specification.

Susan Wynne Roberts holds a Masters Degree in Composing, Analysis and Criticism from the University of Surrey. She has taught music in a wide range of schools, and for some 16 years has been a senior examiner and moderator for A-level composing, developing well-received materials and schemes of work for A-level teachers. She was part of the team writing the current specification for OCR. Sue Roberts is an enthusiastic advocate of 20th-century and contemporary music, her interest in the way composers learn to compose taking her as far afield as Boston and Athens. She now teaches music at Greenhead College, Huddersfield.

Huw Ellis-Williams was brought up in Bangor and studied in Oxford and Exeter. A pianist, organist and part-time composer, he teaches at a comprehensive school in north Wales where he is head of sixth form. Huw has a particular interest in instrumental music of the early 20th century, and in music for theatre and film. He is an examiner for OCR.

Acknowledgements

The authors would like to thank Paul Terry, music series editor, and the following members of the Rhinegold editorial team: Lucien Jenkins, Rose Vickridge and Katherine Smith.

The authors and publishers are grateful to the following publishers for permission to use printed excerpts from their publications:

Introduction

Course overview

There are three units in the AS music examination for OCR:

- Performing Music 1 (worth 40% of the total AS mark)
- Composing 1 (worth 30% of the total AS mark)
- Introduction to Historical Study in Music (sometimes called the 'listening paper', worth 30% of the total AS mark).

OCR stands for 'Oxford, Cambridge and Royal Society of Arts'. It is the organisation that decides what you have to do in each part of this exam, supervises the marking, and awards grades and certificates.

The performing and composing units can only be taken in the summer exam session each year, but the listening paper is set twice a year, in January and June. Most students opt for the June session, since this has the advantage that if you don't do as well as you had hoped it is possible to resit the unit in the following January. Some schools or colleges may let you take the paper early, in the January of your examination year, but if you then want to retake it in June to see if you can improve your mark, you may have to study a new group of set works (see page 59).

Performing

An examiner will come to your centre to hear your performance and discuss it with you. This will happen sometime during the second half of the spring term (March/April) or the beginning of the summer term – you will be told the precise date in advance.

Composing

Your teacher will assess your compositions throughout the course and send an overall mark to OCR with samples of your work (which you will probably choose together). This usually happens early in the summer term. OCR's moderator checks through the work to make sure that all the assessment criteria have been met and that standards are being maintained. If the moderator does not agree with your teacher's assessments (if they're too generous or too harsh) the mark can be changed (up or down). This ensures that your mark is in line with national standards.

Introduction to Historical Study in Music

You will sit a two-hour written paper for which you will be given an individual copy of a CD to listen to on your personal stereo in the exam room. Some of the extracts will be from music that you are not expected to have heard before, but others will be from the set works you have studied. The questions will assume that you are *thoroughly familiar* with *all* of the set works. Make sure at the beginning of the course that you know exactly which **six** pieces you must study – they are listed on page 59.

AS Music is a qualification in its own right. Perhaps you are taking it because you enjoy music and want to broaden your course beyond the subjects that you are planning to take forward to A2. If you work steadily on all three units you will not find it a burden at the end of the course. Performing is usually out of the way by Easter, your composing portfolio will have been submitted at the very beginning of the summer term, and the written examination will not require a lot of last-minute cramming if you have got to know all the music early in your course.

AS is also the first stage of the complete A level in Music: if you intend to go on to A2 you will find that everything you have done at AS has provided you with a firm foundation for the next stage. The A2 units have similar titles and are examined in similar ways.

How this guide will help you

Each unit has a separate chapter which tells you precisely what OCR expects you to do. We have set out all the content in detail and have given you advice on how to prepare.

Although the three units are assessed separately, a common thread runs through them all. This comes from two **areas of study**:

- **Tonality** is about a particular aspect of the language of music and will play an important part in your work for the first half of the composing unit
- **The expressive use of instrumental techniques** is about how to use instruments effectively, particularly in different combinations, and will be the focus of your work for the second half of the composing unit.

Many of the questions in the listening paper will focus on both of these areas of study. 'The expressive use of instrumental techniques' is also relevant to Performing Music 1, particularly if you intend to offer an ensemble or composition in Section C.

The chapters on each unit point out clearly how these two areas of study are involved but there is also a short chapter (starting on page 17) which explains them both. Don't be put off the first time you read this chapter if you don't see immediately how it applies to the music you know best. If you come back to it towards the end of your course you will find that you have learned to understand the chapter through *applying* the various points it contains.

Exercises and practice questions

Throughout this book there are short exercises that have been designed to help you understand how what you have read applies to the music you are studying. At the end of each section on the set works there is a group of practice questions. These are not intended to be mini-exam papers but they will give you practice in answering the sorts of question that are often asked in the listening paper. Working through them will also help you form habits of mind that will stand you in good stead in the examination.

How you can help yourself

Preparing for the performing unit obviously requires regular practice, exercises for the composing unit must be done throughout the course, not all in the last couple of weeks, and learning about the set works for the listening paper will need plenty of time for you to get to know all six pieces really well. So, you need to plan your time – what you will do each week – and draw up a timetable that shows how and when you will complete all the different parts of your work.

But your AS music course is not a set of unrelated hoops that you must keep jumping through. Although each bit has to be examined separately, all your musical activities support one another:

- Being a performer will help you to understand composing and listening
- Being a composer will help you to understand performing and listening
- Being a perceptive listener will help you to understand your own performing and composing better.

When you do any of these things you are being a *musician* and you will gradually discover, as you work through this book, that everything you learn about music is related:

- A detail of how a trumpeter plays in a jazz piece might set you thinking about how trumpets were played in much earlier music, or might give you an idea for your own composing or improvising
- Thinking about the structure of one of the pieces you are going to play in your recital will help you shape the music more convincingly and give you extra practice in analysing harmony and form
- Working out which notes are harmony notes in a melody for your Section A composing coursework will help you to phrase your own performances intelligently and will prepare you for Section A of the listening paper
- Listening to a range of music will help you show an awareness of style and conventions in your own performing.

Because the requirements for Section A of your composing coursework and Section B of the listening paper are fairly precise, we have been able to explain these in plenty of detail to help everyone. But *you* choose all the music you will perform and *you* decide what style of piece to compose for Section B of the composing unit. We can give you quite a lot of general guidance about these and your teachers will give you a great deal of help and encouragement, but the final decisions are yours.

The more you try to make connections for yourself between the different elements of your course, the wiser your decisions will be. If you aim to be a rounded musician who experiences music as a whole, the sooner all the separate elements will fall into place.

Performing

An examiner will come to your school or college to listen to you and discuss your performance with you. The whole performing exam will usually take about 20 minutes.

Section A: Recital (60 marks)

First, you perform a short programme of pieces in which you must be the *soloist*. If you play an instrument which is normally accompanied, like the clarinet, or if you are a singer then you will need an accompanist. The choice of music is up to you, but two or three contrasting pieces should be enough to give you scope to demonstrate a range of skills and show that you understand different styles.

Your programme should not last more than eight minutes. You do not have to perform for that length of time but if your programme is very short it is unlikely that it will let you show yourself off to best advantage.

Section B: Discussion (Viva voce) (20 marks)

Viva voce is a Latin phrase often used to refer to a face-to-face discussion. It means 'with a living voice' and is pronounced 'vee-vah vo-chay'.

After you have played or sung, the examiner will discuss your performance with you. This will not take longer than about five minutes.

Section C: Extended performing (40 marks)

In this part of the examination you have to perform *in a different way from Section A*. You must choose one of the following:

1. Performing a short programme (no more than four minutes long) on a *different* instrument (or voice).
2. Performing in an ensemble or duet. If you play a chordal instrument, such as the piano or guitar, you can choose to perform as an accompanist for this option. Again, a short programme of no more than four minutes in length, is required. Note that:
    - If you had an accompanist in Section A, you cannot do so again for this section and claim that you are now a 'duet' – the examiner needs to hear what *else* you can do
    - The examiner will need to be able to hear your own contribution to the ensemble, so activities such as singing in a choir or playing a part that is doubled by other instruments would not be suitable for this option.
3. Performing your own composition(s) on the *same* instrument or voice that you presented in Section A. At least one other instrument or voice must be involved – you cannot perform an unaccompanied solo for this option. Again, your programme should be no longer than four minutes and it may consist of just one piece or, at most, two pieces. You must hand a fully notated

score of your composition(s) to the examiner before you begin your performance.

4. Improvising. The examiner will give you a choice of starting points and you will be allowed ten minutes to prepare. You may use any instrument (or voice) and are not expected to keep going for more than two minutes. The starting points (some examples of which are shown *right*) will include:

- ➢ Four pitches (without rhythm)
- ➢ A melodic opening (in treble, bass or C-clef) which can be transposed to suit your instrument or voice
- ➢ A short unpitched rhythm
- ➢ A chord pattern (for which you may have an accompanist)
- ➢ A simple poem with an optional melodic opening.

For Section A (and possibly C) you have the option of performing in front of an audience, or in private. The audience cannot stay in the room during the Section B discussion.

Pitch:

Melody:

Rhythm:

Chords:

F	**Dm**	**Gm**	**C**
F⁷	**B♭**	**C⁷**	**F**

Poem:

Music, when soft voices die,
Vibrates in the memory –
Odours, when sweet violets sicken,
Live within the sense they thicken.

Rose leaves, when the rose is dead,
Are heaped for the beloved's bed;
And so thy thoughts, when thou art gone,
Love itself shall slumber on.

(*Shelley*)

Optional opening:

Preparing for the examination

Perhaps you really enjoy performing in public or perhaps you prefer playing or singing informally with just a small group of friends. You might even be someone who prefers creating your own new music, as a composer. Perhaps you really don't like being in the spotlight and enjoy exploring music by performing it out of earshot of other people. As musicians we all have different interests, strengths and weaknesses: it helps if we are honest with ourselves and recognise what they are, then we can exploit our strengths and work steadily on the bits that don't come quite so naturally. It often turns out to have been worth doing after all.

Even the most experienced international performers have nerves. It is rare for anyone to feel after a concert that it was the 'best I've ever done' – there's nearly always something they think didn't quite come off. Professionals are in a competitive world and always strive to be better – better than they were last year, better than their rivals. If you are hoping to take up a career as a performer then you will have to learn to live with this competitive self-criticism – competing with yourself to improve, competing with others to get the job. Being on top of your technique and knowing the music thoroughly must become a way of life for you.

For many of us, though, exploring music through performing it, interpreting it for ourselves rather than only hearing how other people do it, is one of the most enjoyable parts of developing as a musician. It is a way of getting inside music that will help us understand it better and feed our creative imagination as composers. The more we do, the more we will want to do: if we've got a butterfly nature, impatient to sample everything, we flit from composer to composer, genre to genre; if we tend to stick to one thing then we may get more and more deeply interested in one particular composer or type of music. Most likely you are somewhere in between, always pleased when the opportunity to learn a new piece comes along, but with a good handful of old favourites that you enjoy coming back to. Be curious and adventurous in your study. But, when it comes to an examination, *play safe*.

The performing exam is not a series of hurdles set up to see how far round the course you can get before you fall over: it is designed flexibly, to suit everyone, so that not just different instruments or types of voice are catered for, but different interests in music, different personal temperaments and different circumstances as well. On this occasion *you* choose all the music.

The recital

Choose music you feel comfortable with. Discuss it with your teachers and listen to their advice. If you take lessons with an independent teacher outside your school or college make sure they know what the performing requirements are for OCR AS Music – show them this guide.

Don't rely on a single long piece to give you sufficient scope to show a range of skills and understanding. You need at least one other piece of contrasting music. But *how* contrasting? The music you choose should preferably be typical of the repertoire for the instrument. For instance, if you are a pianist, an arrangement of Pachelbel's *Canon* (originally written for strings and keyboard) is not really typical of piano repertoire and will only give you a very limited opportunity to show your understanding of the instrument. It is usually better to play pieces that were designed with the instrument you are playing in mind.

If you are primarily a jazz performer, 'contrasting' does not mean that you have to perform a Baroque work – you can play entirely jazz pieces, but make sure your programme includes music that uses different techniques and is in different jazz styles.

How difficult? You don't need to torture yourself by playing for a full eight minutes at the most extreme limit of your technical abilities. Include something that shows the best that you can do but remember that 'difficulty' isn't only about pyrotechnics – it's also about expressiveness and understanding the music. Choose at least one piece that lets you show what the instrument can express – perhaps a range of tone colours or dynamics, or a very legato singing line. But don't overreach yourself: what goes well when you are relaxed and totally immersed in the music may throw up unexpected problems when you find yourself in an unfamiliar situation.

It is not a good idea to perform without an accompanist if the music was intended by the composer to be accompanied. As the soloist, you need to be able to show that you can coordinate your solo part with the accompaniment. It is your responsibility to make the arrangements for an accompanist. This should be settled well before the examination date so that you have sufficient time to practise together and become comfortable with one another. You need to hear how the accompaniment goes at an early stage of learning the piece, not in the last few days before the exam. You will feel more secure if you know the accompaniment well – it will help to make your performance much more convincing.

If possible, find out which room or hall the examination will be held in, and try to practise there at least a week in advance. If you are a pianist, you will need plenty of time to get used to the piano in the room. If you play or sing with an accompanist, give your accompanist the opportunity to practise with you using that piano, and sort out where you are going to stand or sit so that you have good eye contact between you. Whether you intend to have an audience on the day or not, try your programme out in front of a group of people – friends, relatives or even the public.

Do all this in good time beforehand so that if unexpected problems arise (you find there's a page-turn that you can't manage without the music falling off the stand, or the noise of the air-conditioning hums distractingly through the quiet bits of the music) something can be done about them.

Make sure that you have copies of all your music ready to hand to the examiner. Photocopies may be used. They will be taken away by the examiner for reference, and later destroyed.

Discussion (Viva voce)

The examiner will be interested to find out what you thought about as you prepared each piece – how you made your expressive choices, why you decided to perform a particular passage one way rather than another and whether you think it worked as intended in the performance you've just given. It is not about how many notes you slipped up on, or which bits were too difficult for you – you are not being asked to confess to performing badly – but about aspects of the music that may be less obvious: if you got faster somewhere in the middle of a piece, was this because the composer had marked it *accelerando* or because you felt the music really needed to push on at that particular moment? If the dynamic markings range from ***pp*** to ***ff***, do you think the contrasts were sufficiently effective? What made you put that particular ornament in this phrase? Why did you slur the last two bars that way?

We practise writing about music, learn technical terms, and develop new skills to identify and describe what we hear. But talking about our own performance is not something we are often encouraged to do. In our lessons the usual routine is probably: you play, your teacher listens and then does the talking. And, much of the time, because we respect our teacher's judgement, if they say 'no, play the phrase this way' and then they demonstrate for you to copy, we do it: have you ever asked 'why'? 'Why?' is what the examiner is going to want to discover.

How can you practise for this part of the examination? Start by listening more closely to your friends when they perform and by trying to articulate a more detailed response than you would usually – not just 'that was great', but 'I liked the beginning and the end very much but am not so sure about the middle'. This might lead to a discussion about the effect that their performance had and you could both try to tease out why the outside parts were exciting but that middle bit was boring or dull or just lost momentum. Then invite them for a return match to listen to you and discuss your performance. This isn't enough for the viva, but it's a way to get started thinking about why performances are the way they are – not just because your teachers have said 'do it my way' – and how people sometimes hear what we perform quite differently from what we assumed.

In Section B of the listening paper you will be asked to compare two different performances of a passage from one of the set orchestral scores or be asked questions about the performing style and technique of one of the musicians in the set jazz recordings. Reflecting on your own performing intentions and how effectively they came over in performance is the other side of this coin: when performing, *you* are the interpreter.

Extended performing

The decision about which of the four options you are going to do needs to be taken fairly early. There are a number of practical considerations. Discuss all of the options thoroughly with your teachers before deciding.

If you are thinking of doing option 1 (performing on a second instrument or voice) the choice about which instrument to offer for the Section A recital and which one to offer here can be a tricky one if you are equally strong on both of them. Bear in mind that there are only 40 marks for this part of the examination, while the Section A recital is worth 60 marks. It makes sense to offer your stronger instrument in Section A.

If you want to take option 2 (performing in an ensemble or duet, or as an accompanist), then other performers will be involved and you need to begin to make arrangements for rehearsals as early as possible. Choosing and obtaining suitable music (particularly if your ensemble is not a common combination of instruments) may take longer than you expect. It needs to be something that everyone involved can manage comfortably, but that also stretches you (remember that your part must not be doubled by anyone else).

You also need to give yourself plenty of time to try out your different role – for example, you may never have accompanied anyone before and your soloist's choice of music might challenge you more than you expected. This option puts you into a different relationship with other performers – this time you are not the 'star performer' and you may have to learn some negotiating skills. Be prepared for some setbacks: if you are working with other students, they will be under pressure too, and your examination may not be at the top of their agenda. Agree a manageable rehearsal schedule in good time and stick to it.

If you choose option 3 (performing your own composition), you will obviously need to start drafting ideas, and then refining and completing the actual composition well before the examination.

You may use any instrument, or singing, for option 4 (improvising): it doesn't have to be the instrument you used in your recital. You may have no difficulty deciding which of the starting points is likely to be best for you. If you are a singer, it is sensible to choose the poem; if you're a guitarist, the chords; a drummer, the rhythm. If you play a melody or keyboard instrument, you have more choice. A saxophone player, for instance, might choose the pitches, the melodic opening, the rhythm, or even the chords.

If you play a melody instrument such as the flute and choose the chords as a starting point, you can have an accompanist to play the chords. The accompanist is allowed to practise with you in the ten-minute preparation time but is not allowed to help you with your own improvisation. If you are a keyboard player and choose the chords option, you are *not* allowed to play with another performer.

On the day

You will be told the date of the examination in advance. The examiner will contact your teacher, probably during February, to arrange a time that is convenient for everyone. It may be before the end of the spring term or early in the summer term. Your teacher will draw up a timetable for the day and ask you for details of your programme. It is your responsibility to make sure that your accompanist, if you need one, and any other performers needed for your Section C option, all know the date and time, and confirm that they will be available.

The day before the examination, make sure that everything is organised – copies of the music, music stands, amplifiers and an audience, if you want one. Practise carefully in a quiet frame of mind, and have a good sleep. On the day, keep calm – let yourself breathe. Think positively – the examiner is not the enemy or an alien species. He or she is a musician, probably a teacher and possibly a parent as well, who understands the stress you are under. Very occasionally it may be a surprise when you walk into the examination room to find that that there are two examiners. This is done to make sure that examiners are all marking to the same standard across the country. It doesn't put you under twice as much as pressure!

The whole examination will be recorded – this is a safeguard for you.

The examiner will probably say something welcoming when you come into the room. Listen carefully to everything the examiner says but don't try to read too much into it. If you are asked to wait a few moments between pieces, don't assume that what you've just done was so terrible that a whole essay is being written about it. If you've chosen a programme that goes on too long and the examiner stops you, don't jump to the conclusion that he or she couldn't stand any more – they are probably being very careful to keep to the timetable so that the next student is not kept waiting.

However carefully you've prepared, though, the unexpected can always happen – the fire alarm goes, a string breaks, your accompanist is ill and someone else stands in at the last moment. None of these signals the end of the world. Examiners have these things happen to them in their own day-to-day work as musicians and they understand the extra stress it puts you under. Don't panic – deal with the problem and carry on.

Assessment

Most of us are naturally self-critical about our performing. The desire to improve is healthy and makes us practise but, because we're trying to get it 'right', we sometimes get into a habit of paying more attention to what is 'wrong' than what is going well. The job of our teachers, especially, is to point out what needs attention and how to overcome problems: we may sometimes feel that we can never satisfy them. This can result in our reflections about how we performed focusing too much on the negative aspects, always remembering what went wrong, instead of what worked.

The job of an examiner is different from that of a teacher. It is to notice everything that you *can* do. Right from the start the examiner will be listening in a positive way, giving marks for what you achieve, not taking them away because of things that didn't go well. Examiners work to marking criteria that specify the range of marks available for various levels of performance. As you will see below, it is not just getting all the notes right that matters, there are other aspects of your performance that the examiner will consider.

> The full marking criteria for Performing, along with detailed descriptions of the mark bands, are printed in Appendix B of the OCR Specification.

Recital

Each of the following four categories of assessment is worth 15 of the total 60 marks available for the recital.

Fluency and accuracy

This is an assessment of how well you know the music, how securely you have it in your head. Although it's partly about getting all the notes right, it's more about whether you are confident about where the music is going. If your fingers slip through nerves and the examiner feels that you nevertheless knew what you should have played, the 'fluff' will probably be overlooked.

This also applies if part of your performance involves improvisation: in this case it's not so much about accuracy as whether your musical ideas are fluent and what you play has a sense of direction.

Technical control

You may have learned the music thoroughly and understand a lot about how it ought to go, but can you actually get through it without falling over in passages that are really too difficult for you? This would be an obvious sign that you are not in technical control of your instrument (in this respect the voice is an 'instrument', too).

Although you want to show the very best of what you can do, it is always a mistake to perform music that you are not quite on top of. It will make you extra edgy when you really want to be able to concentrate on all the other aspects that matter. But the examiner will be listening for more than just whether you can perform the correct notes: a wide range of technical skills can be rewarded, some of them quite subtle, like balance between melody and chords or contrasts of tone-colours, as well as more obvious aspects like intonation, pedalling, breathing, tonguing or diction. Try to choose music that allows you to show different technical and expressive skills. If you are a pianist, include something that shows you can use the sustaining pedal, but don't play a whole programme of over-pedalled pieces; if you're a singer, make sure that you show you can sustain a melodic line without help from the piano – don't choose a programme that consists entirely of songs in which the accompaniment doubles the vocal part.

Realisation of conventions

For most of us, the first category of marks, Fluency and accuracy, will be about knowing what the composer wrote on the page – the notes and rhythms. The marks under the third category, Realisation of conventions, are for showing in your performing that you understand other sorts of sign such as tempo and dynamic markings, articulation, ornaments and some of the aspects of music that are not written down – the conventions associated with different types of music. These might include, for instance, playing quavers in a swung style in jazz, or deliberately unevenly (*notes inégales*) in some types of Baroque music, or adopting a flexible approach to tempo (*rubato*) where appropriate in Romantic music. In other words, the examiner will be listening to hear whether you are performing the music in the way that the composer would have expected it to sound.

Aural and stylistic understanding

Do you actually listen to the sounds you are making or are you too busy worrying about what comes next? If your intonation is a bit off, is it because you're not really listening to yourself or because, technically, you can't play it any more accurately? If you came in too soon, was it due to not knowing the music well enough or was it because you weren't listening to the accompaniment? And do you understand the different styles needed for a Bach minuet and a Chopin waltz, or a Mozart aria and a Lloyd Webber song? This is where your *musicianship* really shows.

Discussion (Viva voce)

The better you understand the styles of your pieces and know what to consider when performing them, then the more detailed you can be in your answers and so more of the 20 available marks can be awarded. If you want to, you can illustrate particular points by playing or singing a phrase or passage that you are discussing, *provided that it is relevant.* For instance, you might want to show that you had thought about which notes in a phrase to slur and which ones to detach: it could be appropriate to demonstrate *and then discuss* the differences, in order to explain why you chose to perform it the way you did.

Key phrases in OCR's description of the sort of discussion that would be worth between 13 and 16 of the 20 marks are: 'informed answers', 'clear awareness of expressive choices ... and of their effectiveness in performance'.

Although you will have no idea beforehand what questions about your performance the examiner will ask, you can be sure that there will be no trick questions designed to catch you out. The examiner will be keen to find what you *can* talk about – your communication skills are not being assessed and you will not lose marks just because you stumble over a word. And you have every reason to feel confident because *you* have chosen the music. You are not going to be asked about unfamiliar music. Provided you have thought about what you are doing, and why, as you prepared, and haven't been performing parrot fashion or on autopilot, you should feel that you are on home territory.

Extended performing

The marking criteria for the various extended performing options are mostly similar to those for the recital.

Second instrument or voice

The criteria for this option are identical to those for the recital, except that each of the four categories is marked out of ten rather than 15 marks.

Duet, ensemble or accompanying

This option requires extra aural and stylistic awareness – listening to the other performer(s), coordinating, knowing when to come to the fore and when to blend. In an improvisatory style (like a jazz group) the ability to extend musical ideas in a way that is appropriate to the style also comes into the picture. If a group uses amplifiers, the way they are managed to balance the performance may also be taken into account.

Your own composition(s)

This option is assessed in a similar way to Section B of the composing unit. There are ten marks for the score and the accuracy of its relationship to what is performed; ten marks for the way the composition shows your understanding of the technical and expressive possibilities of your instrument (or voice); a further ten marks for similar understanding of the other instruments or voices involved in the composition; and ten marks for the way the composition shows your aural awareness and understanding of the relationship between all the performers in the combination.

Notice that many of the marks in this option are awarded for composing skills. If composition is your strength, this is the place in the course where you could capitalise on it.

Improvising

For your improvisation there are ten marks available for fluency and form, ten for technical control, ten for imaginative use of the 'stimulus' (the starting point), and ten for your aural and stylistic awareness.

The areas of study

Two areas of study have important roles in underpinning large sections of your AS course – ideas, techniques and various bits of information that relate to them will keep cropping up. You will find it helpful to keep them in mind in almost everything you do. Get your ears tuned in to recognising their relevance in whatever you are performing, composing or listening to.

Tonality

Don't confuse tonality with 'tone colour', which means something completely different. Music that is **tonal** is music that uses one or more keys (as in major or minor).

The word **tonic** refers to the main key of a piece of music and its key chord (chord I). A piece of tonal music usually begins and ends in its tonic key and will probably pass through other keys (**modulate**) in between. These other keys are described as **related** if they contain many notes in common with the tonic – for example, the relative minor shares the same key signature as its relative major key – otherwise they are said to be **non-related**. Relationships between keys play an important structural role in a great deal of the music that you will hear and perform.

The process of moving from one key to another is known as **modulation**. This involves using pitches from the new key and is usually confirmed by a **perfect cadence** (often V^7–I) in the new key.

If the pitches in tonal music all come from the current key, the music is said to be **diatonic**. Pitches outside the current key that are used to add colour rather than to introduce a modulation, are called **chromatic** notes (chromatic means 'coloured').

The major and minor scales of the tonal system are not the only scales used in music. For example, until about 1600 various **modes** were used in European music. Some folk songs are modal, and a number of 19th- and 20th-century composers have used modes in their music to give it a folk or national flavour. Major and minor scales are sometimes thought of as two modes that survived after 1600.

By the end of the 19th century, tonal harmony had become so complex that a clear sense of related keys became increasingly obscured by the use of many chromatic notes. In the 20th century some composers experimented with non-tonal types of scale as a basis for organising their compositions. Today, some music is tonal and some is non-tonal. In your own work for Section B of the composing unit (and for the composing option in Section C of the performing unit) you are free to choose tonal or non-tonal styles, but your exercises for Composing Section A must be tonal.

The rejection of tonality by some composers after 1900 is sometimes described as the 'breakdown of tonality'. Of course, it did not actually die out. Many composers have continued to write in a broadly tonal style, and much western popular music (and even jazz) is essentially tonal in nature.

The word 'western' reminds us that it is mainly in the history of European (and later, American) music that tonality has had such a dominant role. Other civilisations (such as India and Japan) have used different systems. A *raga* sets out the distinctive melodic ingredients from which a long, expressive improvisation can grow. Members of the audience recognise the typical techniques that performers use and appreciate how these are applied in an imaginative and inventive way. Using a common set of conventions, stamped with characteristics of the musician's own personal style, the performer explores the *raga* in an original, unrepeatable musical communication with the audience.

In a similar way, although most of us are unaware of it as we listen to western tonal repertoire, we orient ourselves at the beginning of a piece by fixing the tonic in our ears as 'the place we are starting from', and then recognise and enjoy the way the music travels away from it and comes home again at the end – a satisfying resolution to the story.

As we study the music of the 18th century we will become aware of various conventions – things that were common practice, although never 'rules'. For example, it was common for a piece to begin by making the tonic clear to the listener, perhaps by basing the melody on parts of a broken chord. But it was inevitable that one day somebody would have the idea of starting in a different, more ambiguous way.

In a loose way we often use the metaphor of a language to describe the way tonality works. The parts of this language that you need to learn to handle confidently – the chords, cadences, modulations, passing notes and so on – are a little bit like parts of speech (nouns, verbs, conjunctions). This may be a useful way to think about the techniques and conventions but it doesn't mean that 16 bars of music will have a meaning in the way that a sentence does.

The specific features of western tonal harmony that you must learn to recognise and handle are:

- Major and minor keys in up to four flats or sharps
- Diatonic intervals (major or minor 3rds and 6ths, etc)
- Chords I to VII and their inversions; chords with an added 7th
- Perfect, imperfect, plagal and interrupted cadences, and other common progressions
- Modulation to closely-related keys (dominant, subdominant and the relative minor or relative major)
- Tonal devices such as sequence and pedal.

In the exam, chord names may be given as well as Roman numerals (e.g. VI/Gm).

To use these successfully in your coursework exercises you also need to learn to recognise the harmonic implications of a melody or bass, and to develop a feel for how often the harmonies change (known as the **rate of harmonic change** or **harmonic rhythm**).

All the work you do in Section A of the composing unit is based on this area of study, and it also plays a large part in Sections A and B of the listening paper. Much of the music that you perform will also be in tonal styles, whether from the 17th, 18th, 19th or 20th centuries: understanding its tonal language will help you find suitable ways to shape such pieces expressively.

The expressive use of instrumental techniques

If you took GCSE Music you will have learned something about individual instruments and the sounds that they are able to make, and you will already know quite a lot about the one you play yourself. In this area of study you learn more about performing techniques and how musicians use them for expressive effects. You will also learn about ways of *combining* instruments to produce different textures and sonorities.

Although this area of study is about instruments, if you are a singer it's worth thinking about vocal techniques in a similar way.

As a starting point, see what more you can discover about your own instrument: it may be able to do a great deal more than you are capable of producing on it at the moment. Listen to well-known performers. When you are sure you know your instrument inside out, compare it with similar instruments in terms of its range, registers (the different parts of the range), timbres (tone colours), agility and expressive power.

Your study of three orchestral scores and three jazz recordings for the listening paper will focus a great deal on techniques of performing and on ways of combining instruments. When you come to compose your own music for instrumental ensemble in Section B of the composing unit, the sounds you have been listening to, and the understanding you have gained about how these are produced, will provide you with a stock of techniques that you can draw on. You won't want to compose an 18th-century symphony, or a 1920s' jazz standard – your own musical language will be different – but the textures and timbres you have studied may well be ones that linger in your imagination.

These pieces also provide the focus for your historical study: many instruments in the 18th century looked and sounded very different from the way they do now. You need to know about this. But there is also a great difference in the way composers scored for them at the beginning of the 18th century (Bach) and a hundred years later (Schubert). Even within 50 years (from Bach to Mozart) the instruments themselves were changing. Jazz didn't stand still, either: you will discover differences between the sounds that performers made in the 1920s and only 30 years later, even on the same type of instrument.

In your own performing, too, particularly if you are playing in an ensemble or singing in a choir, get into the habit of noticing who is doing what – playing or singing in unison, 3rds, imitation, contributing to widely- or tightly-spaced chords, throwing a motif from part to part in dialogue, presenting the melody in the lowest part and so on. Also, of course, pay careful attention to details of articulation, dynamics, phrasing and balance.

Composing

The two sections in this coursework unit carry equal marks:

- **Section A: The language of western tonal harmony**

  Seven exercises are required, one of which has to be completed under timed conditions (45 marks).

- **Section B: Instrumental techniques**

  A composition or arrangement is required, written for between four and ten instruments, and with a maximum length of three minutes (45 marks).

Your work for both sections will be marked by your teacher, and samples will be sent to OCR to ensure that the assessment is fair, reliable and meets the required standards.

A great deal can be learned about the craft of composition. Skills and techniques can be studied and acquired in much the same way that a doctor, plumber, engineer or chef gains the expertise they need. Composing involves handling and manipulating the raw materials of music and for this hard work is the critical factor, rather than vague notions of inspiration or natural talent.

At first glance, the two sections of this unit may appear to be quite separate in their demands. The work in Section A will enable you to become familiar with the practices and conventions of tonality – a system that has been the backbone of western music for several centuries. Section B allows for a more personal extension of your composing ideas. Many of the basic concepts studied in Section A will be relevant to your work for Section B whatever style you choose. Both involve studying music by established composers to use as models of best composing practice.

Section A: Western tonal harmony

During the course your teacher will give you a number of exercises consisting of a melody plus the start of the lower part(s). You have to complete the bass part and indicate suitable harmonies. In at least two of these exercises you will need to supply a complete texture in which any inner parts are notated in full, using the given opening as a model.

The melodies in the exercises you actually submit must either be by named composers or be traditional melodies or folksongs – they cannot be tunes specially written for practice purposes.

In the early stages you may well be given short exercises in order to become secure with the basics. However, those you submit should include between eight and 24 bars of your own material, in addition to the given openings.

Near the end of the course you will need to assemble a portfolio of six exercises (plus a seventh, described on the next page), including at least two worked as a full texture. Some other requirements for the portfolio are given in the checklist on page 35.

The type of melody that can be used is wide ranging to enable you to start from your own musical experience and performing abilities. You should aim to cover new ground as you explore the range of music that uses western tonal harmony. Some examples of suitable material might include:

- 18th-century keyboard pieces
- Early Classical string quartets
- Short, simple Romantic pieces
- Hymn settings
- Traditional folk songs
- Simple popular songs from the 19th and early 20th centuries.

It is best to avoid melodies that you are familiar with because these do not allow you to make judgements about the choice of harmony for yourself.

In the early stages your teacher will probably set exercises that have lots of sign-posts and guidance to help you. Later, as you become more confident, you should be able to work independently without hints or prompts. You will probably complete a large number of exercises during the course, from which you can then select six for your portfolio that together best demonstrate your range of skills and understanding.

A checklist is provided on page 35 to help you make sure that your portfolio includes a suitable range of skills and understanding.

Your portfolio must also include a seventh exercise that you have to complete without help and under supervised conditions. This will be done towards the end of your course. You will be given one hour to complete the exercise and you will be allowed to use a musical instrument such as a keyboard or guitar, or a computer (with any assistance disabled) as you work.

Getting started

You may have already learned something about chords and keys from GCSE music or studying for a music theory exam. It is also possible to learn a great deal about western tonal harmony by being inquisitive and curious about the music you play and listen to.

Over the next few pages we introduce some of the basic concepts needed when writing tonal harmony. Further technical detail can be found in the Reference section starting on page 133. If you need more preliminary exercises or clarification, any of the harmony textbooks listed *right* will help.

AS Music Harmony Workbook by Hugh Benham. Rhinegold Publishing, 2008, ISBN 978-1-906178-34-5. This includes exercises designed for OCR AS Music.

Harmony in Practice by Anna Butterworth. ABRSM Publishing, 1999, ISBN 978-1-854728-33-3

The *ABC of Harmony* series by Roy Wilkinson. Boosey and Hawkes

Harmony, Melody and Composition by Paul Sturman. Cambridge University Press, 1983, ISBN 978-0-582331-26-6

The Dynamics of Harmony: Principles and Practice by George Pratt. Oxford University Press, 1984/1996, ISBN 978-0-198790-20-4

To complete the exercises you will need to have a working understanding of:

- Staff notation in bass and treble clefs
- Keys, intervals and scales
- Chords and cadences
- Textures
- Inessential notes (described on pages 25 and 134).

If you can identify these features in the music you perform, it will help reinforce your understanding. Remember that working with chords, bass lines and melodies is a practical activity – try not to think of it as 'theory'. Take every opportunity to understand what is happening by using your *ears* as well as your *eyes*.

The sound of typical bass lines

We often think of melody, bass and harmony as three separate elements in music, but in reality they come packaged together. Melodies are often formed from the notes of chords and bass lines underpin the harmonies. It is possible to play many simple pieces with just the outer two parts – melody and bass – because your inner ear will fill in the harmonies even if they are not played.

Exercise 1

- Choose a short section of music from any Baroque instrumental piece (such as a woodwind sonata) or from a classic popular song (such as Penny Lane by the Beatles).
- Copy out the melody and bass part as accurately as possible, either by hand or using computer software, for two instruments of your choice, for example, violin and cello, or flute and bass guitar. Remember that you will have to transpose any part written for a transposing instrument (see pages 64 and 135). Think carefully about the range of the instruments – you might need to write the parts in a different key, or in a different octave, to be more suitable for your chosen instruments.
- Play the piece in its new instrumentation, noting the strength of these two outer parts.
- Working with a friend:
  - Try out some of the pieces in the *Notebook for Anna Magdalena Bach* by J. S. Bach, with one of you playing the melody and the other the bass part: the majority of the pieces in this collection are written for two parts only (numbers 4, 6, 7 and 18 are all good choices)
  - Sing the soprano and bass parts only from some traditional hymn settings
  - Play only the outer parts from short sections of instrumental works from the Baroque period – you could try some of the movements in Bach's Orchestral Suite No. 3, for example.

In all of these exercises, notice how the bass parts are like melodies in their own right. Even though they generally contain a larger number of wide leaps than the top part, they still create interesting shapes in terms of their movement up and down. Notice, too, how effective the music sounds when the two parts are in **contrary motion** (in other words, when they move in opposite directions).

Chords

Although you will need to work in both major and minor keys, you will probably find it easier to think about chords in major keys to begin with.

A **triad** (three-note chord) can be formed on any degree of the scale by adding a 3rd and a 5th above the bottom note (known as the **root**). Here are the triads of C major:

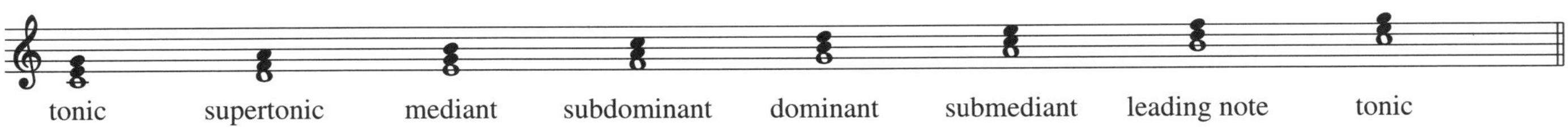

The triads in this example are in **close position** – that is, their notes are as close together as possible. Play them through *slowly* on a keyboard instrument. Can you hear that some sound major and some sound minor? The triad on the leading note is a diminished triad and so sounds rather different.

Chord voicing

Harmony tends to sound more effective if the notes of chords are more widely spaced, in what is called **open position**. The way the notes are distributed is called the **voicing** of the chord, and there are many possibilities when using open position chords – some different voicings of an F-major triad are shown *right*. Notice that F is the lowest note of all the chords printed here. When changing the voicing of a chord, the bass note can be placed in a different octave, but it should remain the lowest note of the chord.

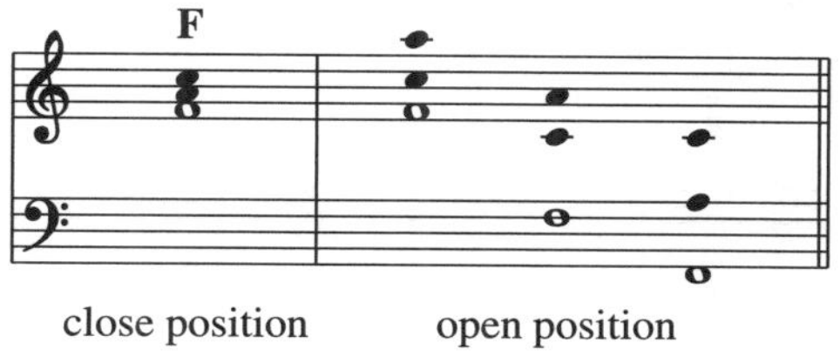

Labelling chords

Using technical names such as tonic or dominant is a cumbersome way to describe triads. A quicker method is to number each degree of the scale and use these numbers to represent the seven different triads available. By convention, Roman numerals are used for chord numbers and in this book we have used upper case for major chords, lower case for minor ones and *italics* for other types of chord:

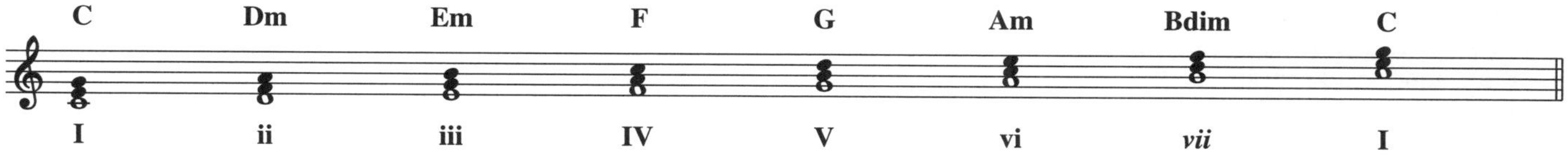

Another way to label chords is shown above the stave in this example – it simply uses the letter name of the root of the chord. If a letter name appears by itself, the triad is assumed to be major. If the triad is minor, the letter name is followed by 'm' or 'min', while 'dim' after the letter indicates a diminished triad.

In both major and minor keys, chords I, IV and V are known as the **primary triads** and should form the backbone of your harmonisation. The most important triad of all is I, the tonic chord, which shares the letter name of the key. You will notice many pieces start and finish on the tonic chord. The next most important chord is V, the dominant chord.

The most commonly used **secondary triads** are ii and vi, although chord iii is also occasionally used.

Why have two methods for labelling chords? Roman numerals have the advantage that they show the relationship of a chord to the tonic. For instance, chord V is always the dominant, whatever key the music is in. Letter names (which are more common in pop music and jazz) have the advantage that they show immediately what notes are to be played – if the chord is C, you play C, E and G.

It is an exam requirement (and good practice) to label your work with chord symbols to show your harmonic thinking. This is especially important in exercises where you write only a bass line without any inner parts.

Get into the habit of being precise with your labels – mark in any inversions (described on the next page) straight away and make sure that each symbol is aligned with the chord to which it refers.

Seventh chords

Adding a 7th above the root of a triad results in a four-note chord called a **7th chord**.

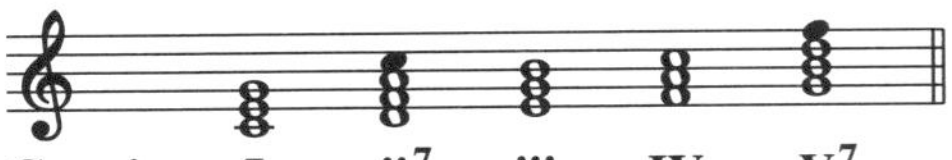

The two most common 7th chords are those on the dominant (V^7) and the supertonic (ii^7). The **dominant 7th** is often used instead of a plain dominant triad in perfect cadences, giving the progression V^7–I, which is one of the strongest ways to assert the tonality of the music. Chord ii^7 is often used as an approach to chord V in a perfect cadence (see *left*).

The 7th forms a **dissonance** (clash) against the root of the chord. This normally resolves by moving down by step to a harmony note in the following chord (F to E in both examples *left*, and also C to B in the second example).

Inversions

The triads on page 23 are said to be in **root position** because the root of the chord is in the bass. If the 3rd or 5th is in the bass, the chord is described as inverted. When the 3rd is the lowest note, we say that chord is in **first inversion**. When the 5th is the lowest note, we say it is in **second inversion**. A 7th chord can also have a **third inversion**, which occurs if the 7th is in the bass.

Root positions *could* be labelled with 'a' after the Roman numeral (e.g. Ia), but in practice it is always assumed that a Roman numeral by itself indicates a root-position chord.

When labelling chords, add the letter 'b' after the Roman numeral to indicate a first inversion or 'c' to show a second inversion (e.g. Vb or Ic). Third inversions of 7th chords are shown by adding the letter 'd' (e.g. V^7d). If you use letter names for chords, label inverted chords by writing '/ ' and then the name of the actual bass note after the chord symbol (e.g. F/A). This is sometimes described as a 'slash chord'. Both methods of labelling inversions are shown in this example:

Chords in root position, and in first or third inversion, are freely used when harmonising melodies, but second inversions are used only in certain special circumstances, as we shall see on page 27.

Exercise 2

Label each of the following triads. Use either Roman numerals or chord letters and show the inversion if the chord is not in root position. The first answer is given.

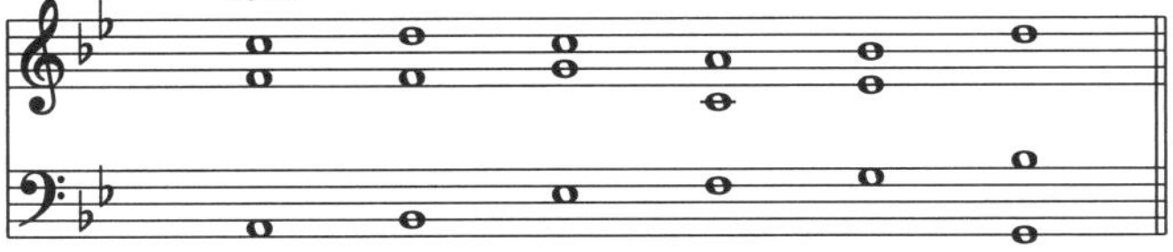

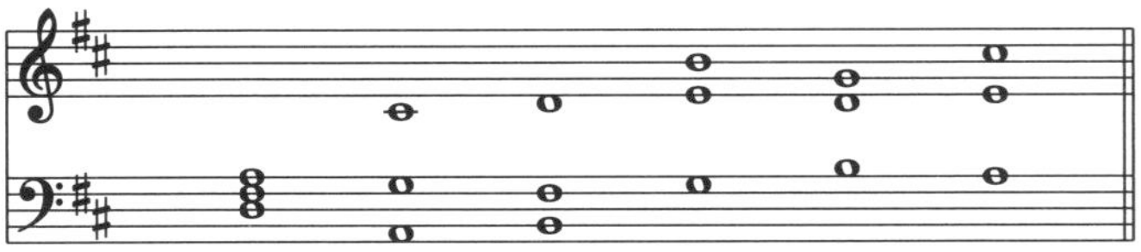

Harmony notes and inessential notes

Some melodies are based largely on **harmony notes** – that is, notes of chords:

J. S. Bach: Minuet in G

This example is in G major, the primary triads of which are shown *right* for reference. The melody implies harmony very clearly. The first four notes in bar 1 belong to chord I, while the next two could be harmonised with chord V (requiring D in the bass). The tonic is emphasised in bar 2, so a return to chord I would be better here than using chord IV (which also contains the tonic). Bars 3–4 are a repeat of the first two bars. In bar 5 there are only two notes, E and G. If we add C as a bass note, we have all the notes of chord IV. Which chord is suggested by bar 6?

	D			G	A		
	B			E	F♯		
	G			C	D		
G major:	I	ii	iii	IV	V	vi	*vii*

Melodies based entirely on harmony notes like this can result in rather angular contours caused by the many **leaps** involved. Most tunes create a smoother outline by including **stepwise movement**:

Petzold: Minuet in G (formerly attributed to Bach)

Here we can see that adjacent pitches (such as G–A–B–C in bar 1) are not all contained within any one chord, so we have to decide which of these are harmony notes and which are not.

We have already noted that many tonal pieces begin with the tonic chord, which in G major consists of the notes G, B and D. Here we have D on the first beat of bar 1, G on the second beat and B on the third beat, so chord I is the obvious choice for bar 1.

But what about the notes printed in grey in this bar? They are not part of the chord and are therefore known as **inessential notes** – a strange term, because they are essential to the flow of the melody, but it really means that they are not essential to the harmony.

There are various types of inessential note – the ones *above* are known as **passing notes** because they pass by step between notes of the chord. Passing notes always move by step – they never leap to or from harmony notes – and they occur in rhythmically weak positions (here on quavers *after* beats 2 and 3) which means that the passing dissonances they create are hardly noticeable.

Sometimes passing notes fall *on* the beat, in which case they are known as **accented passing notes**. These also move by step between harmony notes, but because they occur on the beat, the dissonance they produce against the underlying chord is more noticeable and often very expressive, as in the example *right*, in which the accented passing notes are circled. When the dissonant note moves by step to a harmony note, we say that the dissonance has **resolved**.

Mozart: Rondo K. 485

G major: I ________________

There are several other types of inessential note, details of which are given in the Reference section (page 133).

Using first inversions and inessential notes

Most of the time, your bass notes should be the roots of primary (or occasionally secondary) triads. If you also make use of first-inversion chords and include some inessential notes, you will make the bass line smoother and the harmony more interesting. In this way you will be able to write bass parts that have the well-shaped, melodic character found in the practical exercises recommended at the top of page 21.

We looked at the first four bars of the following melody earlier. Now, with a lower part added, we can see how a well-shaped bass part results from the use of occasional first-inversion chords and the inclusion of some passing notes – note particularly how the bass in bar 8 moves the music forward at a point where the melody itself lacks rhythmic interest:

Petzold: Minuet in G (formerly attributed to Bach)

Play the following harmonisation of a traditional children's song – the melody includes several inessential notes (marked *) but the bass part consists only of the root of each chord:

Traditional: *This Old Man*

Compare the music *above* with the following version. It uses the same chords but inessential notes and extra harmony notes give the bass part a much more interesting shape:

Traditional: *This Old Man*

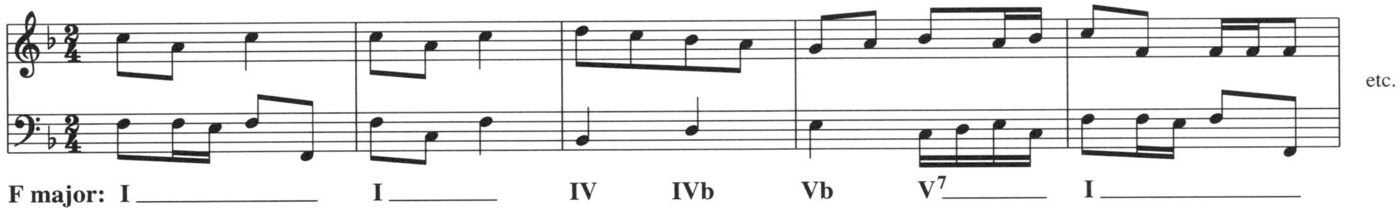

As you can see, once you have worked out the basic harmonies for the melody, including occasional first-inversion chords and adding some inessential notes to the bass part are both excellent ways of achieving musical interest. Additional harmony notes, such as the extra Fs in bars 1 and 5, and the C in bar 2, are also very useful in giving the bass a sense of rhythmic drive.

Phrases and cadences

In music a phrase is a group of notes that form a unit, rather like the way a group of words forms a sentence in speech. Singers and wind players understand this well because the end of a phrase coincides naturally with the place where a breath is taken, just as in speech you would take a breath after a clause or sentence.

Musical phrases often end with a cadence, just as punctuation separates clauses and sentences in English. The two most common types are:

➢ The **perfect cadence** (formed by the progression V–I at the end of a phrase), which can bring a temporary or permanent halt to the music

➢ The **imperfect cadence** (any chord followed by V at the end of a phrase), which gives a sense that the music has more to say and needs to move on.

For more about cadences, see the Reference section (page 133).

In many melodies the phrases fall into lengths of two, four or eight bars. Note that if the tune begins with an **anacrusis** (up-beat) it is likely that most of its other phrases will begin in the same way. This means that the starts and ends of phrases will straddle bar lines, as in the following tune, in which the phrases have been marked with brackets:

Traditional, *The Ash Grove*

G major: **ii** ______ **V** __ Imperfect cadence **Ic** __ **V** **I** Perfect cadence

If you count the beats in this example, you will see that the first two phrases are each 12 beats long, which equates to four bars of $\frac{3}{4}$ time, so we still refer to these as four-bar phrases.

Using second inversions in your exercises

Second inversions are also known as $\frac{6}{4}$ chords because, as shown *right*, the upper notes are a 6th and a 4th above the bass note. This way of indicating chord notes comes from **figured bass** notation (see *right*).

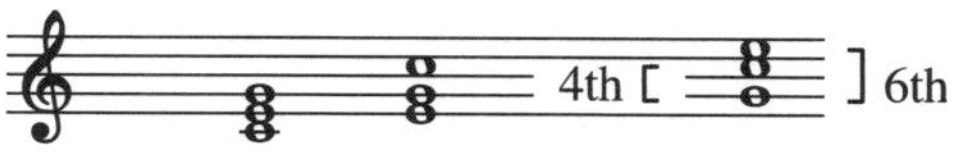

C major: **I** **Ib** **Ic**

In **figured bass** numbers and other symbols below the bass part show the notes needed to form the rest of the chord. It is a more complicated way of indicating harmony than Roman numerals or chord symbols, so we haven't used it in this guide, but most good textbooks on harmony explain how it works.

Second inversions tend to sound harmonically unstable, as if they want to move on to another chord, and are therefore normally used only in two special circumstances:

1. Chord Ic can be used immediately before a perfect cadence, forming the progression Ic–V–I, as seen in bars 7–8 of the example *above*. This is known as a **cadential $\frac{6}{4}$** and can be a good way to create a strong cadence. In a cadential $\frac{6}{4}$ progression, chord Ic falls on a strong beat and the dominant note forms the bass of both Ic and V. Sometimes the second of these repeated bass notes drops down an octave, shown by the bracketed note in the next example, resulting in the familiar shape shown in the bass part at the cadence:

J. Bishop, *Illsley*

2. A second inversion can also be used when the music passes between the root position and first inversion of the same chord, as shown *left*. Incidentally, both of these progressions work equally well in reverse: Ib–Vc–I and IVb–Vc–IV. This type of second inversion is known as a **passing $^6_4$** and always comes on the weaker part of the bar.

Both types of second inversion, passing and cadential, appear in the following example – notice how smoothly the inner parts move:

Traditional, *All Through the Night*

Harmonising a melody: preliminary exercises

- When starting an exercise, first identify its key.
- Then write down the five most useful chords for that key in the way that you prefer, either on a stave or in the form of a grid (as shown *left*).
- Next, sing or play the melody through several times and then, once you are familiar with it, mark in the phrases and choose chords for the cadences at the end of each phrase.
- Use your aural awareness and knowledge of harmony to make choices about the remaining chords. Remember to look out for clues in the melody, as we observed earlier. You may need to try several options for some chords in order to find the best choice for the particular context.

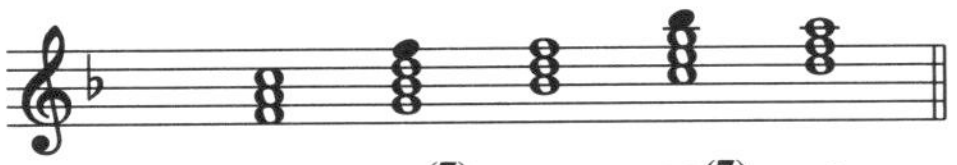

7th		(F)		(B♭)	
5th	C	D	F	G	A
3rd	A	B♭	D	E	F
root	F	G	B♭	C	D
F major:	**I**	**ii(7)**	**IV**	**V(7)**	**vi**

Exercise 3

Harmonise this melody by writing the name of one suitable chord in each box. Think carefully about which chord would work best before the perfect cadence in the final bar.

Traditional, *London Bridge*

Harmonic rhythm

The rate at which the harmony changes in relation to the melody is called the **harmonic rhythm**. In hymns and chorales (German hymn tunes) chords usually change on almost every beat of the bar. But in other types of melody the harmony usually changes less frequently – perhaps two chords a bar, perhaps only one, and in some cases the same chord may extend over two or more bars.

Up to half of the exercises in your portfolio can be harmonisations of hymn or chorale melodies, if you wish. But the remainder should show different rates of harmonic change where you have to think carefully about the best places to make chord changes.

Sometimes the rate of harmonic change will increase at important cadences. Look back at *The Ash Grove* on page 27 and notice that only one chord per bar is needed for most of the tune (and a tonic chord could be used for the whole of bars 1–2) but two different chords are needed in bar 7 at the point where the perfect cadence is reached. There was also an increase in the harmonic rhythm in the last bar of the melody used in Exercise 3. Use your ears to help decide the places at which the harmony needs to change.

If the tune includes rests on strong beats (as in the melody for Exercise 4 *below*) you will usually need to place a chord on these beats, since it rarely sounds good if the accompaniment as well as the tune is silent on a strong beat.

Exercise 4

Choose suitable chords for the following melody by writing appropriate symbols in the correct positions above or below the stave. The first two bars have been completed for you – notice that each chord lasts for two crotchet beats, and that a chord is placed on the rest at the start of bar 2. There is no need to increase the harmonic rhythm at the final cadence in this example.

Writing a bass part

After deciding on the chords to use, you need to write a bass part. As we noted earlier, this will be more effective if it proceeds in contrary motion to the melody as far as possible. It is also a good idea to include musical interest in the bass at any points where the melody has a long note or rest.

As you add the bass you may want to change some of the chords you selected earlier, in order to give the bass line a better shape, or perhaps you may decide to use a first inversion rather than a root position chord (remember that *second* inversions should not normally be used except as cadential or passing $^6_4$ chords). If you change any chords, remember to alter the chord symbols as well.

Shown *left*, on the staves marked (a), are some possible chords and an outline bass part for the first two bars of the melody in Exercise 4. Did you notice that this same two-bar chord pattern can be repeated in bars 3–4?

The outline bass part is very dull, but this is where melodic decoration can come to the rescue. Staves (b) and (c) show just some of the ways you could make the bass part more interesting by using a passing note (*P*), additional harmony notes (*H*) and auxiliary notes (*A*).

In the exercises for this paper you will be given the start of the bass part, which should help suggest the type of decoration that would be appropriate to use in the rest of the working.

Working in full texture

For the purpose of these exercises, 'full texture' means at least three notes sounding together.

At least two exercises will need to be completed in a full texture, meaning that as well as a bass part and chord labels you will need to add one or more inner parts. This could take the form of an accompaniment for piano or guitar, or the exercise could be for a group of instruments such as a string quartet. The texture to use will be shown in the opening bars of the exercise.

Four-part harmony

Another popular way of working in a full texture is to write for voices in four-part harmony, notated on two staves, as shown *left*. The melody, or soprano part, is written on the treble stave with note stems pointing up. Below it comes the alto part, written on the same stave but with stems pointing down. Next comes the tenor part, written on a bass stave with stems pointing up, below which comes the bass part, with stems pointing down.

When writing in four-part harmony, at least one note in each triad has to appear twice in the chord in order to produce the required total of four parts. We speak of such notes as being **doubled**. There are some basic rules of good practice about which notes to double in a chord:

- The root is generally the best note to double. Alternatively, the 5th can be doubled (and is often the best option in second-inversion chords).
- The 3rd of a primary triad should *not* be doubled (doubling the 3rd in other triads is fine).
- A chord may contain the root in three of the four parts, as long as the 3rd of the chord is present in the remaining part.

When spacing chords in four-part harmony, note that:

- The interval between the soprano and alto, and between the alto and tenor, should never be more than an octave.
- The interval between the two lowest parts (tenor and bass) can be more than an octave.

A useful tip for achieving good spacing is to keep the tenor part high. Tenors are used to notes up to G above middle C, so don't be afraid to make use of leger lines above the bass stave when writing your tenor parts.

Part writing

Look again at the excerpt from *All Through the Night* on page 28. Notice how the inner parts are quite static and avoid unnecessary leaps, yet all parts lead from one note to another in a musical way. This horizontal aspect of harmony is known as **voice leading**, and is an important concept in traditional harmony. Some examples of good and bad practice in part writing are given on page 134.

Chord progressions

So far, we have looked at chord progressions for cadences, such as Ic–V–I and ii–V, but now it is time to consider which chords best lead up to such cadences. They will obviously need to fit the given melody, but there is often a choice of chords and some are likely to produce stronger harmonic direction than others.

The strength of progressions such as ii–V–I lies in chords whose roots fall in 5ths. We can extend this principle to longer chord progressions, but first it is important to understand that a falling 5th is effectively the same as a rising 4th. Using entirely falling 5ths results in an angular bass line that could descend below the range of the instrument or voice concerned, as on the upper stave *right*. To avoid this, falling 5ths usually alternate with rising 4ths, as on the lower stave *right*.

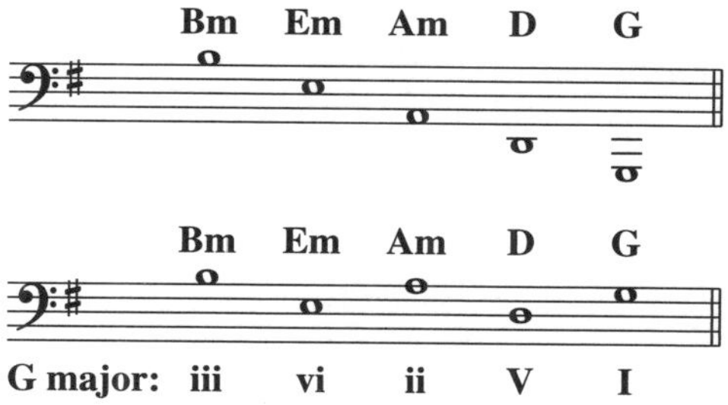

In the next example, a progression of falling 5ths leads to a perfect cadence in bars 3–4. The melody of the first two bars is repeated a step lower in free **sequence** to form the last two bars. Notice how the chords and bass follow this same sequential pattern:

Bart Howard, *Fly Me to the Moon* (simplified)

When working on your own exercises it is often a good idea to try working backwards from a cadence in order to find a progression like this that effectively leads into that cadence.

For more on falling-5ths progressions see **Circle of 5ths** on page 135.

Exercise 5

In the last movement of Mozart's Clarinet Concerto (one of your set works) the composer uses a diatonic circle of 5ths in bars 167–175. Write out the bass part on manuscript paper and study the way in which both falling 5ths and rising 4ths are used. Between which two notes does Mozart use an augmented 4th rather than a perfect 4th?

Working in minor keys

Each major key is partnered by a minor key which has the same key signature and is known as the **relative minor**. Its scale starts three semitones below the tonic of the relative major and it needs an accidental to raise its seventh degree (the leading note) by a semitone:

To raise a degree of the scale that is a flat (such as B♭) you need a natural sign to turn it into B♮. But if the note to alter is a natural (such as G) then you will need a sharp to raise it by a semitone (G♯).

E♭ major

C harmonic minor

There are two different varieties of minor scale. The one printed *above* is called the **harmonic minor** and, as its name suggests, is used primarily for writing harmony in a minor key.

The other is known as the **melodic minor** and its ascending and descending versions are slightly different. On the way up, both the sixth and seventh degrees need to be raised by a semitone but on the way down, both notes are restored to their unaltered states:

C melodic minor

The name 'melodic minor' indicates that this version of the minor scale is often preferred for melody writing because it avoids the awkward sound of the augmented second between the sixth and seventh notes of the harmonic minor.

Because chords have to fit with melodies, they sometimes have to include notes from the melodic rather than harmonic minor scale, and so there are sometimes different versions of the same chord that can be used in minor keys. Here are the ones you are likely to need most frequently:

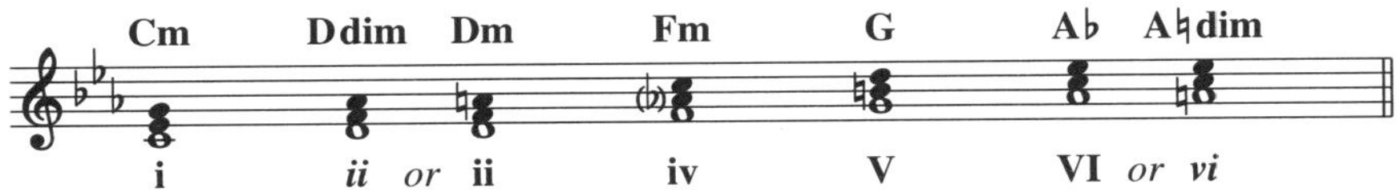

The notes of the harmonic minor produce a diminished triad on chord ii, whereas the notes of the ascending melodic minor result in a minor triad. If you need to use a diminished triad, a good tip is to remember that it works best in first inversion with a doubled 3rd – the same applies to chord *vii* in both major and minor keys.

Your portfolio should include at least one exercise in a minor key. The melody should be clearly minor – avoid folk tunes such as *Scarborough Fair* and *Greensleeves* that are modal rather than minor.

Altered triads are possible on any degree of the scale in a minor key – even the final tonic chord is sometimes major at the end of a minor-key piece. However, chord V is normally used in its major form (as shown *above*, with the raised leading note as its 3rd), especially when it appears as a chord in a cadence.

A complete exercise

We can show only one complete exercise here. Examples and exercises in a variety of textures can be found in the *AS Music Harmony Workbook* by Hugh Benham (see page 21).

By now you may be wondering what a complete exercise, suitable for inclusion in your portfolio, might look like. Bearing in mind the range of options mentioned on page 21, the following exercise is only one example of many possibilities. The given material is the complete melody plus the whole of the four-bar introduction. The actual working is 16 bars long and is modelled on the three-part keyboard texture of the given opening:

Name ....

Date ....

The Ash Grove

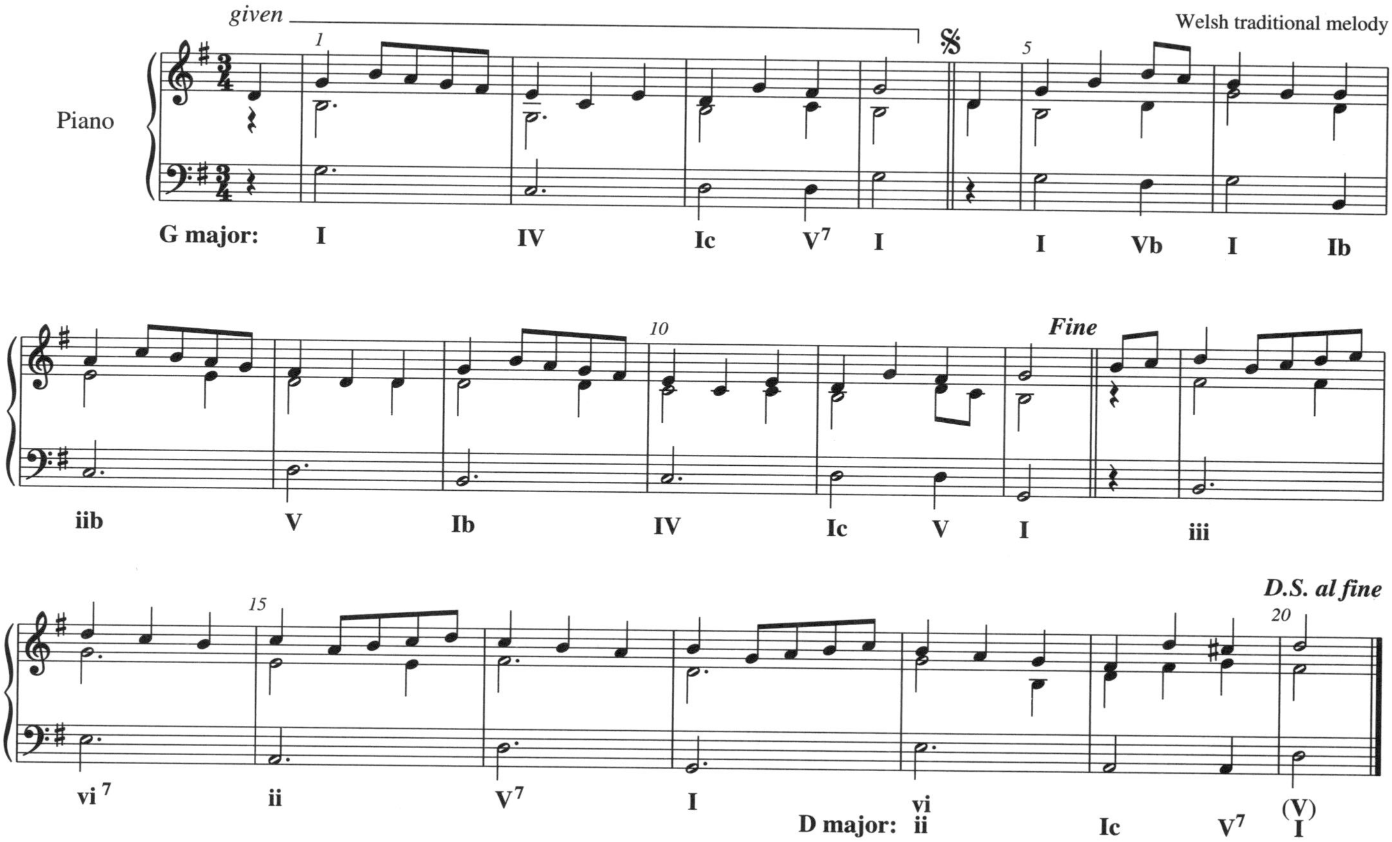

The instruction *D.S. al fine* at the end tells the performer to repeat the music from the sign (𝄋) until the word *Fine* in bar 12.

Notice how the bass and chords follow the descending sequence of the melody in bars 13–18, just as they did in the example on page 31, not deviating from the pattern until bar 18.

Modulation

There is a **modulation** (change of key) to the dominant (D major) in bars 19–20 of the exercise *above*, signalled by C♯ in the melody and confirmed by a perfect cadence in the new key.

The E-minor triad in bar 18 prepares the way for this modulation by acting as a **pivot chord** – a chord that is common to two keys. Here, E minor is chord vi of G major, the key we are leaving, and chord ii of D major, the key we are approaching. Notice how the modulation is shown in the chord symbols. They make it clear how the music has moved from one key to another and how the chord in bar 18 acts as a pivot chord.

You should include at least one exercise in your portfolio that shows you know how to modulate. Modulations are likely to be to closely related keys, such as the dominant, subdominant or relative minor.

You will need a second modulation in order to return to the tonic. Here, the chord in bar 20 is chord I of D major, but also chord V of G major. It thus prepares the way for the return of the tonic key when the music repeats from bar 5.

Assessment

Of the 45 marks available for your portfolio:

- 20 are awarded for harmonic language (your choice and pacing of chords, and use of effective progressions)
- 15 are awarded for technique (creation of a strong bass line, continuity of texture from the given opening, understanding of issues such as modulation and avoidance of technical problems such as consecutive 5ths)
- 10 are awarded for the clear and accurate use of notation.

The exercise on the previous page should achieve a good mark because:

- The bass has a strong shape resulting from the use of primary triads in root position, along with occasional secondary triads and inversions
- The inner part moves smoothly, avoiding awkward intervals, and the bass moves largely in contrary motion to the melody
- The chord progressions lead effectively to the cadences and include correctly resolved dominant 7ths, appropriate use of chord Ic, modulation and (in bars 13–17) a falling-5ths pattern in which a harmonic sequence (iii–vi^7–ii–V^7) nicely reflects the melodic sequence in bars 13–16
- The work has been checked for good voice leading, with no consecutive 5ths or octaves between melody and bass.

Maintaining momentum and a sense of harmonic direction from the start to the end of each phrase is especially important. With experience and observation of how harmony functions in your set works, you will become more confident and successful in the harmonic choices you make.

Preparing your portfolio

Exercises may be hand-written, providing they are legible and accurate, and it doesn't matter if they include your teacher's marks and comments – in fact, they may well help the moderator. It is often better *not* to write out neat copies since new mistakes easily creep in when copying.

Make sure that the given material is clearly identified in each exercise, so that the moderator can see exactly what you have added. If you have used notation software to produce a printout of your work, you could indicate the given bars with a highlighter pen or perhaps include a printout of the initial template you were given for each exercise.

Remember that it is possible to make mistakes even when using a computer notation programme. Notes of chords in each part must be vertically aligned and notes must have correct accidentals – for example, writing A♭ rather than G♯ is an error if you are in the key of A minor. Correct beaming of grouped notes is also important.

All exercises must include chord symbols – either Roman numerals (with inversion letters) to show the chords, or letter names (with slash chords to show inversions) or figured bass. You should not use guitar tab because this shows finger positions rather than actual pitches, but you can add tab above the stave notation if you find it useful when trying out your work.

Your teacher will assess your portfolio and it will then need to be available for moderation if required. It should be clear to the moderator which of your exercises form the core evidence upon which assessment has been made. It is not necessary for you to include preliminary work. Make sure that access to your exercises is easy; a simple paper clip to group your sheets together is more effective than plastic pockets.

The following checklist can help you make sure that when you select the exercises to include in your portfolio, all requirements for Section A of the composing unit have been met.

Portfolio checklist

- ☐ At least six exercises completed during the course
- ☐ One further exercise completed under supervision towards the end of the course
- ☐ All exercises contain between eight and 24 bars of added material
- ☐ Bass line and chord symbols completed in all exercises
- ☐ Bass line, chord symbols *and inner part(s)* completed in at least two full-texture exercises
- ☐ A range of keys represented, with at least one exercise in a minor key
- ☐ Examples that show the correct use (and resolution) of chords V^7 and ii^7
- ☐ Examples showing the correct use of second inversions
- ☐ Example(s) including modulation
- ☐ Correct identification of cadences and cadence approaches
- ☐ Notation checked for accuracy and legibility.

Section B: Instrumental techniques

For this part of the unit you can write *either*:

- A composition for 4–10 instruments *or*
- An arrangement of a lead sheet for 4–10 instruments.

Whichever you choose, you will need to submit a full score of your work in staff notation, a commentary and a recording. If you choose the arrangement option, you should also submit the original lead sheet that you used.

Although most of the following information refers to composing, much of it also applies to arranging. Your work will be judged by the same criteria whichever option you choose. Some specific issues that affect arrangements are discussed on page 48.

Introduction

The area of study, The Expressive Use of Instrumental Techniques, takes centre stage in this part of the composing unit. You will need to understand the characteristics of a range of instruments and the ways in which they can work together. Your own experience as a performer and your knowledge of the set works will form a good starting point for this. The word 'expressive' in the area of study is of particular importance – in composing we express our thoughts and feelings, sometimes in a surprisingly objective and methodical way, via the medium of a musical instrument. To express is to *communicate* and to be successful your composition must have a real sense of communication for its listeners.

Which instruments can I use? The composition must be for 4–10 instruments, which can be acoustic, amplified or a combination of both. You can include voices if you wish, but only in addition to the 4–10 instruments, and you should note that you can only gain credit for your writing for instruments.

> You need to show that you can write for instruments, not their synthesised equivalents. For example, a flute part should be designed to be played on a flute, not a synthesiser. However, you are allowed to use synthetic sounds in the final recording, if necessary. If you and your teacher are unsure what is permissible, contact OCR and ask.

You have a wide choice of instruments (but see *left* for some important exceptions). However, it makes sense to write for:

- A group of fellow students who will be available to try out your work as it progresses, and to rehearse and perform it for the final recording
- A group of instruments that will sound well together.

How long should the piece be? The upper limit is three minutes, but there is no penalty if your work does not precisely meet this requirement. You should aim to say everything you want to say, musically speaking, within this time. Be disciplined and avoid rambling on for longer than necessary, but avoid a piece that is too short as it won't allow you to show the full value of your ideas and expertise.

Style You can write in any style you wish, but it is easier to work in an idiom with which you are really familiar. All composers have learned from existing music by playing it, listening to it, studying it and arranging it, only gradually developing their own composing voice. It is important that you too study the music of others as a way of developing your own skill as a composer. In the commentary it is especially important to give details of all the pieces you have studied that are relevant to your composition, and explain precisely how they have informed your own work. Think about the music that you know:

- Take an audit of the music you listen to – which styles do you like and know well, what gaps are there in your current listening experiences?
- Borrow scores of your favourite pieces from your school or library (or, if available, download them from the internet). Identify and copy out the melodies, short motifs, rhythms or chord progressions that you find particularly interesting. Keep a journal of your musical discoveries.
- Take stock of your current repertoire as a performer. Discuss the range of music available for your instrument or voice with your specialist teacher if you have one.
- How might the repertoire you play in any ensembles to which you belong be relevant to your ideas for composing? Consider forming a group to experiment with composing ideas or to perform arrangements of interesting music.

What will be examined?

The 45 marks available for your composition or arrangement are split into four categories, each of which we will explore in detail over the following pages:

- **Materials (10 marks)** are your basic ideas, the building blocks of your piece – the rhythmic patterns, melodies, bass parts, chord progressions and so on
- **Use of medium (15 marks)** refers to your understanding of the particular qualities of the instruments you have used and the ways in which you have combined them
- **Technique (10 marks)** is the skill with which your materials have been constructed on a small scale and then developed, combined and connected to form a larger structure
- **Communication (10 marks)** is the way in which you have conveyed your ideas in both the score (which needs to be complete and accurate) and the recording (which needs to give an effective interpretation of your music).

As there is no restriction on the style of your work, remember that the examples given in the rest of this chapter indicate only *some* of the possibilities open to you.

Materials

Melodic materials

One of the most important elements in many types of music is melody. Your work in Section A of this unit will help you to understand the various ways in which melodies can be assembled. The character of a melody is shaped by its rhythm, pitches, overall contour and pace. Strong melodies often consist of mainly step-wise movement with occasional leaps. Think about the opening of the well-known tune *Greensleeves* – the melodic intervals reflect this basic principle and we can also hear that the leaps are ones with strong harmonic implications (chord notes are marked *):

The linear intervals created as a melody moves from one note to the next can have a profound effect on its character. John Williams' theme for *Schindler's List* is deeply expressive whether or not we know the subject matter of the film. Another melody, Beethoven's *Ode to Joy* has a somewhat measured and noble quality. Consider the extent to which these characteristics are related to the use of stepwise and angular movement within the melodies.

Both pitch and rhythm play a part in determining the character of a melody as can be heard in Henry Mancini's *Pink Panther* theme:

The climax of a melody is often found between two-thirds and three-quarters of the way through, as in the example *below*. It doesn't have to be loud, high-pitched and joyous – it could be low, quiet and mysterious.

Even when melodies are not particularly distinctive in either pitch or rhythm, we can see invention in the way they unfold. Notice how the melody of the folk song *The Water is Wide* (*below*) slowly expands the range of notes outlined in each of its four phrases. There is a firm sense of upward direction in the unfolding melody as it moves toward the high point at bar 9 before finally coming to rest in the fourth phrase:

A good way to write a melody is to start with a short, memorable **motif** which can be repeated, manipulated or contrasted to form a phrase. More importantly, such motifs can become a source for development in different ways later in the piece.

The next example is built on a four-note motif. When the motif is repeated, its opening interval (an octave) contracts to a 7th. The second half of the phrase starts with another repetition of the motif (in which the opening interval is now reduced to a 5th), but this time the motif is extended to eight crotchet beats in length, thus balancing the combined length of its first two appearances. The graph-like lines above the stave show the contour of the melody, which consists of a long descent to balance the upward leaps at the start of the motif:

Exercise 6

1. Construct a balanced melody of four phrases in an inverted arch shape () in which the lowest point is reached in the third phrase. Base it on a short motif that is modified and then either extended or contrasted, like either of the previous two music examples.
2. In your study of the set works, you will notice that composers often present two contrasting melodies that are complementary in nature. Compare and contrast the theme played by oboe and clarinet in bars $13–20^1$ of the first movement in Schubert's *Unfinished* Symphony with the cello theme in bars $44–53^1$ of the same movement.
3. Copy out the melody in bars 1–6 of the Air from Bach's Orchestral Suite No. 3 in D. Show the contour of this melody by accurately drawing its contours above the stave, in a similar way to that used in the previous music example.
4. Investigate the ways in which motifs are used and distinctive themes constructed in as many of the following works as possible:

   Delius: *La Calinda*, from Three Orchestral Pieces
   Bizet: Farandole from *L'Arlésienne* Suite No. 2
   Grieg: *Peer Gynt* Suite
   Bartók: Concerto for Orchestra, third movement
   Reich: Three Movements for Orchestra (1986), second movement.

Bass materials

We have already noted in Section A (page 22) that bass notes underpin the harmonic possibilities of a piece of music. A bass part may have a strongly melodic character, as happens in music of a **contrapuntal** texture where each of the voices has an independent line. In rock music, **riffs** in the bass part can play an important role too; they may be the foundation upon which an entire piece is built.

A **ground bass** is a repeating bass part above which different melodies unfold. While it is a device often associated with Baroque music, it can be very effective in other styles of music. Pachelbel's well-known Canon in D is built upon a simple ground bass that is played 28 times, while a series of increasingly complex melodies unfold in canon above it. Other examples to study include the Ricercare from Bach's *Musical Offering*, Britten's Passacaglia from *Peter Grimes* and *When God Created the Coffee Break* from the album *Strange Place for Snow* by the Esbjörn Svensson Trio.

Your study of jazz recordings will allow you to investigate a range of bass lines and their relationship to the harmonic framework. You may have studied the 12-bar blues for GCSE and now at AS level you will learn how standard bass patterns can be presented in various interesting ways to suit 8-, 16-, 20- and 32-bar structures.

> Clearly notated examples of typical walking, rock and Latin bass lines can be found in the Appendix of *Jazz Styles: History and Analysis* by Mark C. Gridley. Prentice Hall, 1978/2008, ISBN 978-0-136005-89-6.

Exercise 7

If you are studying the first group of jazz recordings, listen to the way the bass moves from static passages to sections of greater activity in *Black Bottom Stomp*, and explain how the walking bass in *Jumpin' at the Woodside* maintains interest when the harmony remains unchanged over several bars. If you are studying the second group of jazz recordings, compare the bass parts in the A and B phrases in the AABA choruses of *It Ain't Necessarily So* – what difference in role is there between the double bass and tuba?

A weakness in many AS compositions is a bass part that doesn't go beyond simply reinforcing the harmony and so lacks real interest in its own right. Yet, in a work like Miles Davis' *So What*, the bass player is entrusted with the most important motivic material from the start. In addition to the good practice you will find in the orchestral scores and jazz recordings you study, the music of the following bass players may be instructive:

Jack Bruce (Cream)
Jaco Pastorius (Weather Report and solo)
Michael 'Flea' Balzary (Red Hot Chili Peppers)
Victor Wooten

Rhythmic materials

Rhythm is a key ingredient in establishing the character of a piece. Steady crotchets, robotic quavers, lilting triplets, snappy dotted rhythms, lively syncopations, rapid semiquavers or asymmetric patterns such as those created by the heavy string accents in Stravinsky's *Rite of Spring* – each can create a different mood.

Dance-based music is usually associated with particular rhythmic patterns and regular phrase lengths: slow duple time for stately pavans, fast compound time for jigs, moderate triple time for waltzes, duple-time phrases that begin halfway through the bar for gavottes (as in the example on page 38) and so on.

The Latin music associated with the countries of South America has enjoyed great popularity in a variety of musical contexts. For example, many of the numbers in Bernstein's *West Side Story* are based on Latin-American dances. Such influences have been heard in popular music and jazz for many decades. More recently, the music of the *Buena Vista Social Club* (1997) revived interest in Latin-American music and a new album (*Supernatural*) released by Carlos Santana and younger artists in 1999 is convincing proof that its popularity continues.

John Adams: *Short Ride in a Fast Machine*

Louis Andriessen: Instrumental III from *M is for Man, Music, Mozart*

Graham Fitkin: *Servant*

African drumming and Balinese gamelan as well as the music of the medieval French composer Pérotin have influenced the music of Steve Reich. The compositions of Philip Glass and Peter Gabriel's film scores similarly show the rhythmic influences of other times and cultures. The short works listed *left* provide further fruitful opportunities to experience ostinati and driving rhythms at work.

Remember that your initial rhythmic ideas will need refinement and control as you continue to work on your composition.

Harmony materials

If you write in a tonal idiom you will have a feast of listening materials on which to draw, including and beyond the set works. But there are other ways to organise pitch such as serial or non-serial atonality and modality. Most popular music is either tonal or modal, and so beginning with a chord progression is often a good starting point for many student composers.

Listen to Barber's Adagio for Strings and excerpts from Michael Nyman's film scores for examples in which the harmonic materials dominate the musical content. For both these composers, the richness of their harmonic language is influenced by music of the Baroque and Classical periods. Nyman openly acknowledges his borrowings from Purcell and Mozart.

You will learn in your study of the set works how the organisation of pitch is closely connected with the musical structure. The keys or tonal centres often provide an important means of defining a section, which may move on to develop initial ideas or provide a complete contrast.

Use of medium

Marks in this category are awarded for how well you have written for the instruments you have used – are the parts playable and do they exploit the character of the instrument? Is there interest in all of the parts – or are some condemned to dull accompaniment patterns with little melodic interest?

In preparation, you will need to research all you can about the instruments you use – discuss with the performers the various tone colours available at different dynamics, any special effects that might be possible, how much time is needed to insert a mute or take a breath on a wind instrument, which chords are possible on a guitar, which musical features (such as glissandos, trills or fast passages involving low notes) might prove difficult, what different types of tonguing, bowing or vibrato sound like, and so on.

We have used the clarinet as an example in the following section, since you will be taking a detailed look at clarinet writing when you study Mozart's Clarinet Concerto, but similar principles apply to all instruments.

The clarinet has a wide range of over three octaves, but there is more to take into account than just the highest and lowest notes. The range of a clarinet can be divided into three registers, each with a distinctive character and a special name. The following example shows the *written* pitches – the most common type of clarinet, the clarinet in B♭, sounds a tone lower than written:

See page 135 for more about the clarinet in B♭.

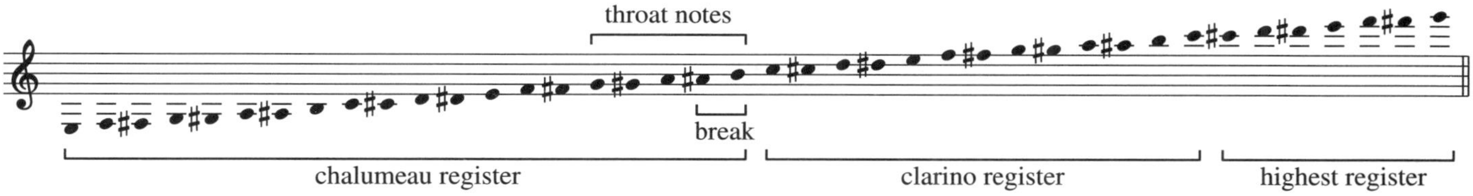

The chalumeau register is relatively quiet but highly individual – the timbre of the lowest notes is rich and dark and is sometimes described as 'oily'. Less-experienced players should be happy in the chalumeau register, since beginners normally start with notes in this part of the range. However, the 'throat notes' marked *above* are more problematic – they tend to be pale in sound and are difficult to play in tune. It's usually better to avoid using them in exposed solo passages, although an inventive composer could exploit these features for a particular effect.

'Chalumeau' was the name of the clarinet's predecessor in the Baroque period.

The clarino register is bright when played loudly, but it can also be warm and expressive at lower dynamic levels.

'Clarino' (or 'clarion') refers to a high trumpet part – the type of music for which the early clarinet (literally a 'little trumpet') seemed suited to play.

Just before the clarino register comes the 'break' – the point at which a difficult change of fingering is needed for the transition between A♯/B♭ and B♮. Moving between these two notes is not just a question of skilful finger technique – the amount of air and the push from the diaphragm are also important because this is the point at which the column of vibrating air moves from being its shortest to its longest. Wise composers take note of this and avoid rapid passages that hover around these two notes.

The highest register tends to be shrill and penetrating, although accomplished clarinettists can play quietly and sweetly in this part of the range. The upper limit depends on the skill of the player – the top G shown on the previous page is fine for proficient players (professional clarinettists can manage even higher notes than this) but if your player is of a more modest standard, then E, three leger lines above the treble stave, is a safe working limit.

Web link

For information on extended techniques for the flute, see www.johnmcmurtery.com/ET/

A variety of special effects (sometimes called 'extended techniques') is available to clarinettists. It is possible to bend pitch (to create a blue note) or even produce a **glissando** (a long, continuous glide in pitch) by carefully shading the holes and keys with the fingers – effects exploited by George Gershwin in his *Rhapsody in Blue*.

Accomplished players can also produce effects such as **flutter tonguing** (rolling an 'r' while blowing to produce a rasping sound), **multiphonics** (which can either mean playing two notes at the same time, one of which tends to sound distant and ghostly, or can mean singing into the instrument while playing), **key clicks** (a quiet percussive effect produced without blowing), **air notes** (blowing into the instrument without producing tone) and **slap tongue** (a percussive attack caused by a violent release of the tongue, more associated with the saxophone, but possible in the low register of the clarinet).

Effects of this sort are often associated with avant-garde music and you may wish to make use of them in this or another appropriate context. But don't forget that more standard techniques can offer a huge amount of variety – write out a short tune (or just a scale) and ask your clarinettist to play it slurred, staccato, sforzando and legato-tongued to see how these various types of attack differ.

The wide range of the clarinet means that it can function as a melody instrument, bolster the middle of the texture, or even act as a bass instrument. In the following example, one clarinet plays low accompaniment figures in the chalumeau register while the other sings expressively in the clarino register:

Mozart, Symphony No. 39 in E♭, Trio

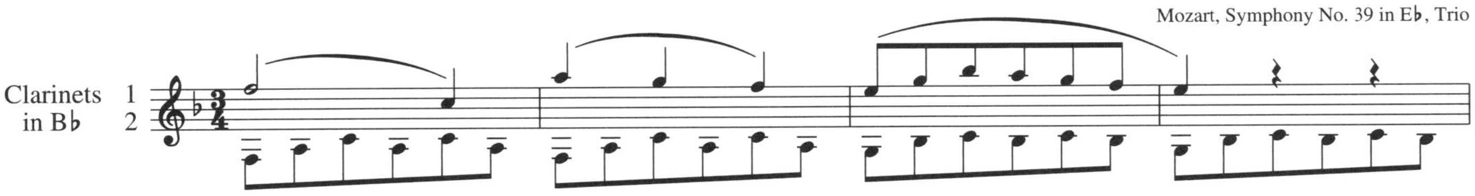

Remember that the least effective range of the clarinet lies in just the place you might be tempted to write for it – on the stave itself. A good rule of thumb, both for clarinet and flute, is that if you are not making regular use of leger lines (above and below the stave for clarinet, above only for flute), then you are not writing in a way that will show the instrument at its best. The clarinet can play rapid scale passages and can jump dramatically between registers, effects that have been exploited by many composers, especially Weber:

Clarinettists have a range of ways to vary their attack. Its single reed has the capacity for smoother, less edgy articulation than double-reed instruments and can respond to a range of tonguing, from detached to staccato, with many shades between. The effortless way in which the instrument can navigate difficult twists and turns is no doubt the reason why Prokofiev used the clarinet to characterise the cat in his *Peter and the Wolf*.

Exercise 8

In the third movement of Mozart's Clarinet Concerto:

1. Identify a short section in which the clarinet remains in the chalumeau register and a section where the clarino register is mainly used. Identify a continuous passage that uses the widest possible range of the instrument in this movement.
2. Write out the clarinet part in bars 57–72 *at sounding pitch*, including any articulation markings your score contains. Listen to at least two performances and write in the score any differences you hear. Try to hear the *precise* way in which the semiquaver runs are variously tongued, slurred or more sharply articulated in a staccato manner.
3. Mozart gives his orchestral players some performance directions in terms of dynamics but he knew his original soloist well enough to allow him liberty to shape the movement with few explicit instructions. With a pencil and score in hand, identify the main dynamic landmarks you hear in a recording of a performance of your choice. Make a comparison with a second recording.

When researching the capabilities of the instruments you intend to use, remember that there are many sources of advice:

- The performers you are going to use and any specialist tutors who may teach in your school or college
- The classical and jazz set works you are studying, which include many examples of good practice
- Books such as those listed *right*
- Internet sites, such as www.bbc.co.uk/orchestras/guide/ www.soundjunction.org ('instruments and voices' section) and www.nyphilkids.org ('instrument storage room' section) – the last of these is aimed at children but all three include detailed examples to audition and useful factual information.

Orchestral Technique: A Manual for Students by Gordon Jacob. Oxford University Press, 1931/1982, ISBN 978-0-193182-04-2

Orchestration by Cecil Forsyth. Dover Publications, 1914/1986, ISBN 978-0-486243-83-2

Orchestration by Walter Piston. W. W. Norton, 1955, ISBN 978-0-393097-40-5

Rock, Jazz and Pop Arranging by Daryl Runswick. Faber Music, 1993, ISBN 978-0-571511-08-2

Exercise 9

Undertake a thorough investigation of an instrument you would like to include in your composition. Use a range of resources including books, scores and the internet; be sure to listen to some of the music that will be recommended in the sources you use. Prepare a five-minute presentation for other students, including a practical demonstration if you have researched an instrument that you play yourself.

Technique

Marks for technique are awarded for small-scale structures (the way that phrases are organised) and for the form of the entire composition. In both cases, the key to success is to balance unity with variety – too many new or unconnected ideas and your piece will not seem integrated; too much repetition and it risks becoming predictable and boring.

Small-scale structure

From your study of Mozart's Clarinet Concerto you will know that some composers build melodies from short, balanced units. The rondo theme in the last movement is built of phrases that are each the equivalent of two bars in length:

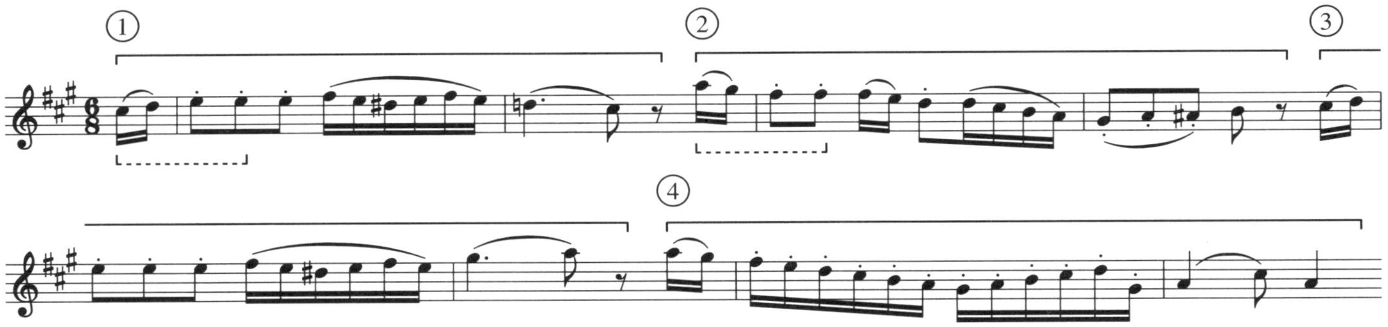

Phrase 1 starts with an anacrusis and Mozart uses this to unify all four phrases of his theme. Phrase 2 moves the music forward and yet it doesn't sound totally different because Mozart starts it with an inversion of the opening four notes (shown by a dashed bracket). The phrase ends with an imperfect cadence, thus making it clear there is more to follow. Phrase 3 is similar to phrase 1, but it ends with an interrupted rather than a perfect cadence. Phrase 4 starts in the same way as phrase 2, but now the semiquavers continue, culminating in a satisfying perfect cadence to conclude the theme.

The phrases are balanced because they are of equal length (each equates to two bars) and because they are arranged in complementary pairs (questions and answers). This balanced phrasing is typical of music from the Classical period, but the idea of creating a melody by building on what has gone before is an excellent way of balancing unity with variety and can be applied to many different styles of music.

Exercise 10

Evaluate the small-scale structure of some melodies you are working with in Section A of the composing unit and of some of the melodies you play in your favourite pieces.

Developing ideas

Creating music from a few tiny melodic cells can be one of the most fruitful ways of composing, since they offer the potential for development in all sorts of ways, both later in the phrase and later in the piece. Composers have often used standard techniques to enable a melodic idea to grow from the briefest of starting points. Motifs are often repeated before being transformed in some way. Possible transformations include:

Transposition	Moving the motif uniformly to a new key
Tonal sequence	Repeating the motif at a higher or lower pitch but adapting intervals to stay in the same key
Interval alteration	Keeping the general shape but reducing or enlarging the size of some intervals
Fragmentation	Using just part of the motif
Extension	Continuing the motif beyond its previous end
Decoration	Replacing notes with several shorter notes
Simplification	Replacing several short notes with a single long note
Inversion	Reversing the direction of all the intervals: e.g. rising 3rds become falling 3rds
Augmentation	Systematically increasing the length of notes
Diminution	Systematically reducing the length of notes

Motif:

Transposition:

Motif repeated in sequence:

Interval alteration:

Fragmentation:

Extension:

Decoration:

Simplification:

Inversion:

Augmentation:

Diminution:

Other techniques include retrograde, in which the order of the notes is reversed (so G–B–C–G–F–E becomes E–F–G–C–B–G) and retrograde inversion, in which the notes of the retrograde version are also inverted. However, these types of transformation are not easily perceived by the listener, and tend to be used mainly in particular styles of music such as serialism and sometimes minimalism.

Composers frequently combine different types of transformation – so a motif might be fragmented and then that fragment might be used in sequence, inverted and decorated.

What this all boils down to is that you really don't need many ideas for a well-integrated composition – it is what you do with them that counts!

Large-scale structure

Assembling your composition means paying close attention once again to the balance between new, repeated and varied material. You also need to bear in mind the intention of your piece. For example, club dance music is designed to be very repetitive and so may not give you much opportunity to show the range of skills required in a three-minute piece. On the other hand, the structure of a film score is often determined by the action on screen, which can result in a collage of ideas that don't have a *musical* structure beyond the context of the film. In minimalist music, ideas often unfold gradually, in which case the structure is more about the rate at which these ideas change than actual contrast.

It is important not to be too ambitious in a composition of three minutes' duration – simple structures often work best. If you choose something like ternary (ABA) form, remember that the middle section should offer a contrast – but it shouldn't sound like a totally different piece. And when the A section returns, resist the temptation to 'cut and paste' the opening bars – consider how it can be modified to create a convincing conclusion, aiming for a structure such as ABA^1, perhaps adding a short coda as well.

Extending your listening

Listen to preview tracks and radio programmes on the internet.

Use a library: CDs, DVDs and scores are often available for loan from public libraries and possibly from your school or college. Some libraries offer free access to resources such as the thousands of tracks in the Naxos Music Library.

Use the radio: *Late Junction* on Radio 3 offers an eclectic mix of global music, new classical and jazz. *Hear and Now* is the main contemporary music programme on Radio 3. Listen to *Composer of the Week*. Classic FM offers a wide selection of enjoyable, largely mainstream classical repertoire.

Many individual music tracks can be purchased cheaply via internet sites.

Support live musicians by going to concerts in your local area.

Your study of the set works will help you to understand how keys relate to structure, setting up areas of contrast, expectation, tension and release. Remember, too, that other music that you perform or enjoy listening to can offer ideas on how to structure a piece. For example, think about whether the typical features of a popular song (introduction, verse, chorus, bridge and coda, with perhaps the use of a modulation to lift the final repeat of the chorus) might be adapted to form an instrumental composition.

Pay particular attention to the ways in which composers move smoothly from one idea to another, often making connections between them on the way. Notice the techniques used to avoid losing impetus in a piece, such as overlapping the last chord of a cadence with the first note of the next section, or filling a long note or rest at the end of a phrase with some relevant decoration in a different part.

Make sure that the structure of your own work is aurally clear, and draw attention to it in your commentary. A lack of purposefulness in structure, harmonic language or technique cannot be excused by the explanation 'I want it to sound like this'. If the evidence points to random musings without design and control, your work will not score well under technique.

Exercise 11

1. Compare the return of the slow section at the end of the overture in Bach's Orchestral Suite in D with its first appearance at the start of the work. How does Bach avoid it sounding like an exact repetition?
2. Identify and explain the ways in which contrasting ideas contribute to the musical structure of a piece you are currently playing or singing.
3. Analyse the structure of a popular song of your choice and show how the form used might be adapted for instrumental composition.
4. Invent a short motif that has the potential to be transformed in some of the ways listed in the table on the previous page and then use some of these methods to turn it into a complete theme.

Communication

When your composition reaches an audience, the process of music communication will be complete. A written score enables your work to be performed by others and a recording will provide one possible representation of your work in audio format.

The score

The layout of the score should follow accepted conventions – refer to published scores to check standard practice. Accuracy of pitch and rhythm are essential. If you use notation software check that the correct clefs have been used to avoid unnecessary leger lines, that key signatures and accidentals are correct, that short notes are beamed correctly and that long notes are not confusingly expressed as multiple tied notes. Find out how to set a small but readable stave size for the score in order to minimise page turns and avoid wasting paper. Check that notes on leger lines don't overlap with the staves above or below.

Note that guitar tablature cannot be offered as an alternative to staff notation. Proficiency in the use of staff notation is a requirement at AS level.

Make sure that you add full performance directions, including dynamics, phrasing, articulation, marks of expression and tempo directions. These markings not only increase the likelihood that performers will play your piece as you want them to, but they will also provide evidence that you have thought about the varied ways you can use the instruments to the full in your composition.

Note that it is perfectly acceptable to submit a handwritten score for your final document. Accuracy, legibility and attention to detail are the main issues whichever format you adopt.

Check that the staves have been labelled with instrument names, and give your piece a meaningful title which accurately reflects your intentions.

Improvisation

If any sections of your composition use improvisation they should at least be notated in outline. Non-notated improvisation by any performer other than the composer is not credited as composition.

The recording

There are various options for recording your composition:

- A live performance with intended forces – while this takes time to rehearse and record, it can offer the most realistic realisation of your ideas in most styles of music
- A multi-tracked performance in which the various parts are recorded separately and then mixed down into a stereo format
- A mixture of intended instruments and substitutions for any that are unavailable, such as playing a double-bass part on a synthesiser
- A performance on the piano or other keyboard instrument – this means playing from a piano reduction of the score that will usually omit some of the detail
- A sequenced version of the composition – this should be fully edited to represent the expressive intentions as effectively as possible
- A mixture of sequenced and live parts – even the inclusion of just one live instrument can transform the often mechanical realisation produced by music software.

Don't worry if your live performance contains some mistakes, as this is preferable to a perfect but bland computer recording that does not convey any life or expression.

It makes sense to consider your options right from the earliest planning days of your composition. If you write for fellow students you will be able to try things out as your ideas develop as well as getting valuable advice from the players themselves. You can use other students, teachers and friends to perform your piece if you wish. You do not have to play in your own composition, but you do have to take charge of the rehearsals and recording; after all, this is part of the assessment and so needs to be your own work.

Check your recording on a conventional playback system and keep backup copies of both the recording and the score. You should not submit data files or use other formats which require specialist equipment or programmes. When you hand in your final folio for assessment, you should include your individual recording for your teacher to listen to and assess.

Arrangement of a lead sheet

If you choose to submit an arrangement instead of a composition you must include a copy of the lead sheet containing the melody and harmony indications with your final submission. The assessment will focus on what you have *added* to this given material and the way in which it has been manipulated and creatively presented. Note that much of the information in the preceding sections is as relevant to arranging as it is to composing.

Many arrangers will have specific jazz or band line-ups for the realisation of their ideas but less conventional uses of medium are also possible and acceptable. Issues for consideration include:

- **Variety of texture**: try to avoid an obvious succession of solos and think about how different pairings or groups of instruments might feature. Try to be imaginative in inventing suitable parts for the rhythm section, especially the bass.
- **Melodic additions**: these could include countermelodies, riffs and fills between phrases.
- **Melodic alteration**: such as adapting a theme to a different style or using anticipations and syncopation to energise the theme.
- **Harmonic realisation**: not just voicing the given chords but also varying the harmonies with added notes and substitutions.
- **Structure**: be imaginative in extending standard structures by adding extra material – an introduction, an ending, interesting features in short solos, new sections that complement the style of the given material.
- **Instrumentation**: ensure that you use your chosen instruments in an idiomatic way, exploiting their possibilities to the full.
- **Tempo and key**: consider altering the original and varying the key and/or tempo at some stage in the arrangement.

It is important to supplement your listening by hearing arrangements relevant to your chosen style. The prescribed recording of Gil Evans / Miles Davis, *It Ain't Necessarily So* from *Porgy and Bess* (set for exams in June 2011 and later) is an excellent place to start since it reveals a highly creative approach to Gershwin's original material. *Summertime* and *Bess, You is My Woman Now* from the same album (details on page 59) are also well worth studying. Inventive treatments of this type are likely to do much better than bland transcriptions in which there is no attempt to transform the spirit of the music with the individual fingerprint of the arranger.

Further listening suggestions

Cannonball Adderley's Fiddler on the Roof. Capitol Jazz 542309-2. This includes arrangements of eight numbers from the hit broadway show.

John Coltrane: *My Favorite Things*. Atlantic 1361-2. A legendary re-working of a song from Rodger and Hammerstein's *The Sound of Music*.

The Bad Plus: *These are the Vistas*. Columbia 510666-2. Two tracks are described as deconstructions of enormous hits: *Heart of Glass* and *Smells like Teen Spirit*.

The commentary and the brief

You will need to give details of your composing brief and provide a commentary about your work, on a form provided by OCR. This information shows how you tackled your work and, if done well, can help maximise your marks.

The brief is a concise statement of your composing intentions and you will find it very helpful to discuss ideas with your teacher. The statement may need to be adjusted as work on your composition progresses. Being open to the twists and turns of the creative process may mean your definitive brief will only be certain once the work is well under way.

The purpose of the commentary is to provide:

- An outline of the *specific pieces* you have listened to and the ways in which they influenced your composing
- An explanation of the processes you used to create the work.

Try to be very clear about the way in which listening connects with your composition – you may want to use short notated snippets of music in your description to explain this.

Simply saying something like 'I really liked the sound of the violin (or guitar) in piece *X* so I decided to write for this instrument' is not very helpful. It is much more informative to say something along the lines of 'I really liked the sound of the violin in the first movement of Bartók's String Quartet No. *X*, in particular the extended techniques in the use of the bow such as …' (and then supply the details), or 'The sound of the lead guitar in Satriani's album *Crystal Planet* opened my eyes to a range of timbres and playing techniques …' (and then give precise details).

When describing your composing process, try to avoid giving a blow-by-blow account of what is clearly self-evident in the score. A simple, analytical explanation of the main ingredients of your work is important, as is an explanation of the decisions you made about structure, repetition, contrast and so on. Concentrate on explaining *what* you did and, more importantly, *why* you did it.

Spend time on the commentary and aim to show that you are familiar with a range of relevant listening that has influenced your work. Remember that the commentary will provide evidence to the examiner that will help them decide the marks you get for Materials.

Finally

Whether you are a composer or arranger, take pride in being the author of something that is your very own. Be sure to know the fine line between unacceptable plagiarism and legitimate, acknowledged instruction from others. Give yourself plenty of time to rework your ideas; you may need to produce several versions of an idea before you get it right. Take the advice of performers around you and work with instruments from the very start of the composing process if you can. You have many options and must give yourself time to consider carefully the choices you make as the work progresses. If a live performance is a realistic possibility for you, enjoy the sense of achievement that such an opportunity brings. If you are able to add a live element to a technologically realised portrayal of your work you may find this can also be very satisfying. Allow time for rehearsal, revisions, and unanticipated technical problems. Above all, take responsibility for a written and audio representation of your work that expresses your musical ideas with accuracy, clarity and integrity.

Introduction to historical study in music

Exam overview

The examination for this unit takes the form of a written paper that lasts for two hours (15 minutes preparation time and 1¾ hours writing time). The question paper is accompanied by a separate booklet (called an 'insert') containing scores and a CD of recorded extracts of music. You are allowed to play the recordings as many times as you wish, within the time available, on a personal CD player equipped with headphones. The paper is in three parts:

Section A (30 marks)

You will be asked several short aural questions based on two or three recorded passages from a piece of *instrumental* music. The music will not be taken from your set works – it may well be from a piece that you are unfamiliar with. You choose extracts from *either* the period 1700–1830 *or* from popular music from 1900 to the present day. You are advised not to spend more than 45–50 minutes on this section.

Section B (40 marks)

There will be two groups of questions:

- The first group is based on a recorded extract and score from *one* of the three orchestral set works that you will have studied (**25 marks**)
- The second group is based on *one* of the three jazz recordings that you will have studied (**15 marks**).

You must study both sets of music. The detailed list for each year is shown on page 59. Check this carefully to make sure you study the right works for the year *and* session (January or June) that you intend to take the examination.

Section C (20 marks)

You will have to write an essay in answer to a question on an aspect of the background to one or more of the six set works that you have studied. There will be three questions for you to choose from. Although you only have to answer one question, some of the questions are likely to require writing about more than one of the works.

You are allowed 15 minutes at the start of the examination to read through the paper, look at the scores for Sections A and B, find the tracks on the CD and get yourself organised. Most importantly, this gives you a chance to *listen to all your extracts* – make the most of this opportunity.

Content

The study of any sort of history involves gathering evidence, establishing facts and interpreting them. Music history is no different: it depends on analysing evidence.

Evidence

Evidence includes contemporary documents (that is, documents from the day) such as newspaper advertisements, reports and reviews, letters, such as those to or from the composer or others involved in a first performance, bills, records of fees paid to performers or instrument makers, and the diaries and journals of informed commentators of the time. Other types of evidence may be less reliable. For instance, biographies – even when written soon after the composer's lifetime – may include misremembered facts or the biographer may have let his own views influence the account.

The primary document, if it still exists, is often the composer's autograph score or an original recording of a jazz work – although composers sometimes revise their works for later performances and jazz musicians frequently devise new versions of previously recorded tracks. Sometimes an early published edition in which the composer has made corrections or other annotations (such as suggestions to a pupil for fingering or realising ornaments) may provide evidence. Further clues to how 18th-century music was performed may come from 'teach yourself' books that were published at the time – these were often weighty treatises that explain in detail the performing conventions of the day. The 18th-century composer, Quantz, wrote one on playing the flute, and Mozart's father, Leopold, wrote about playing the violin.

> An 'autograph score' is one in the composer's own handwriting.

Facts

A straight chronology of events, or list of dates when music was composed or first performed is one type of starting-point. Another might be geography – where were things happening? Whether a composer was Austrian or French, or whether a jazz band was playing in New Orleans or New York, might have made a difference to the style of the music. Who taught whom? Which performers are known to have worked together? Piecing together the trail that leads from one musician to another can cast light on our understanding of their music.

> When writing about dates, be careful not to confuse years with centuries. We live in the 21st century, but the years begin with 20, not 21. Similarly, 1780 is not in the 17th century but in the 18th century.

Interpretation

The evidence is analysed, hypotheses are explored, and judgements are made. The purpose is to help us understand why the music is as it is, how the composer would have expected it to sound and what it is 'about'. To answer these questions we need to apply different sorts of analytical skill.

In the examination you will be expected to have understood what is involved in gathering and interpreting historical evidence, and to be able to discuss what is known about the background context of the set works (particularly in Section C). You are not expected to do your own historical research – that is done by the writers of academic textbooks – but doing some additional reading will help you form a better picture in your mind. Some useful sources are listed in this guide.

> Although informal research is often done on the internet today, it is important to remember that most web sites are not subjected to the rigorous checking and editing applied to academic textbooks. Information found on the web may therefore not be accurate.

You are expected, however, to have studied the music itself very closely, first-hand, and to be able to discuss it using technical language. To do this successfully you will need to develop specialised analytic skills. These are discussed at the end of this section.

Reception

'Reception' is a word used to describe how a work was regarded by audiences, critics and performers of the day as well as how perceptions of a work have changed over time. For instance, in the 19th century some writers referred to Mozart as 'divine' because his gifts were thought to be so great. Twentieth-century writers have looked more closely at the human being, the man behind the music, and found a much less 'divine' personality. This has not meant that his music has been valued less, but it does mean that our perception of what we hear and how we make sense of it may be different in the 21st century.

How the first performance of a piece of music is received depends on what the audience are expecting. If they are familiar with the style they may appreciate the work's inventiveness and what it expresses. Eighteenth-century audiences were used to hearing much new music, often specially composed for the occasion. If a work didn't sound up-to-the-minute they might complain that it seemed old-fashioned and stale, although if it was very innovative they could be shocked.

Study of the history of music in the mid 18th century was confined to a few enthusiasts. Awareness and appreciation of old music began to develop among musicians towards the end of the century and to spread more widely during the 19th century. By the 20th century it was common for orchestral concert programmes to give pride of place to the music of earlier composers, especially those who were by then recognised as great masters, while performances of new music became less common.

Conversely, jazz and popular music still depend on a constant stream of new music, although they too have their histories and there is a keen appreciation of landmark performances of the past.

Transmission

How does music become known to an audience beyond those present at a first performance? Today communications are immediate. Until the advent of photocopiers and computers with music-notation software, parts had to be copied by hand. Copying played an important role, too, in how students, composers and connoisseurs got to know new music. This was a slow process. But, by the end of the 18th century, the demand for music to perform at home had fuelled rapid growth in music publishing and composers in the next century were increasingly able to earn part of their living from sales of their music. But there was no copyright protection, so pirated editions and handwritten copies would quickly circulate if a first performance had been a success.

In the late 19th century, greater prosperity enabled more people to purchase pianos and sheet music to play at home, both coming down in price as a result of industrial manufacturing processes. This was followed, in the early 20th century, by radio and recording which widened the audience for music further still. No longer was

> Connoisseurs (people with an expert understanding of an art) have been as important in music as in any other art form. For instance, many aristocrats were accomplished performers on instruments and some composed as well. They often had enough interest and wealth to commission new music, employ musicians and to accumulate libraries of music to perform and study. Composers frequently dedicated music to them. Sponsorship is still important, although today funds are more likely to be channelled through charitable trusts, broadcasting companies and government agencies such as Arts Council England.

it necessary to journey to a large city to hear celebrated performers, or to pay high box-office prices – everyone could access the latest music cheaply and immediately. Recordings by different artists (or the same ones on different occasions) could easily be compared. Popular audiences became increasingly knowledgeable about the music they liked.

Reception and transmission are also aspects of the study of the history of music that you may be asked about in Section C.

Analytic techniques

Some people find the term 'analysis' rather off-putting, but it simply means discovering how music works – an essential skill for any musician. It is about finding out how music makes its impact and it also helps us to understand how styles and genres change over time, to trace the influence of one sort of music on another, to explain what appears to be a radical innovation – perhaps dispelling myths that portray it as one man's revolution overnight – and to categorise trends and identify common characteristics.

You will need to develop analytic skills for the listening paper. In Section A you will be applying these to understanding an extract of *unfamiliar* music, listening and answering questions 'on the hoof'. In Section B you will already know the music well and will be expected, therefore, to be able to answer more probing analytic questions.

What is involved in analysis? First, you need a keen ear – you must be able to distinguish one instrument from another, one part from another, the treble, the bass, the keys, chords, cadences, repetition and variation, structure, and so forth. Then you need to be able to identify specific techniques used in the music, such as sequences, pizzicato, imitation or pedal notes, and to give them their technical names. Finally, you need to be able to describe and explain how the music works in your own words.

Writing about music needs practice. There are many short exercises in this guide designed to help you build up the skills you need in order to be able to answer confidently in an examination. Work through them all slowly and don't skip any. Then you will be ready to get the greatest possible benefit from working through complete practice tests.

Section A

This section of your exam is not just a test of aural perception: you will need to understand musical notation, know technical terms and be confident about identifying keys, chords and cadences. The recordings are accompanied by a skeleton score and you will be asked to write in a missing phrase of melody, notate part of a bass line, name chords or identify ornaments.

A skeleton score gives an outline of the music, often on two staves, with enough detail for you to follow it as you listen, but it also has quite a lot of information missing. Bar numbers and CD timings are printed in the score to help you follow the recording.

Whichever extract you choose (1A on instrumental music from the period 1700–1830 or 1B on instrumental popular music from 1900 to the present day) it will usually consist of two or at most three short passages separated by short breaks. These will be labelled 'passage 1i', 'passage 1ii' and 'passage 1iii', and will all be from different sections of a single piece of music. Sometimes the second and third passages will be actual variations of a theme that was given in the first passage but, more often, they will simply use *some* of the same material as the first passage but in slightly different ways. As well as questions related to tonality and the expressive use of instrumental techniques, you might also be asked about the ways in which the later passages vary material from the first one.

Tonality

Whichever extract you choose, its musical language will be tonal. The questions are a test of whether you can really hear the techniques you have been learning and using in your exercises for Section A of the composing unit.

The scores will be straightforward, so that the notes are not too dense on the page or cluttered with too many other symbols. The examiners are more interested in what you hear and whether you understand the tonal style than in setting you complicated writing tasks. But you do need to be able to read treble *and bass* clefs confidently, and to be able to notate pitches and common rhythmic patterns accurately, because you will be asked to notate short passages (on the score) in both clefs. Most importantly, you must be sure of your *keys*, not just recognising them from key signatures at the beginning of the score but hearing and identifying modulations that happen in the course of the extract. Making sure you can do this should be an important part of your preparation.

There is no list of keys that you should know for this question paper, but in Section A of the composing unit you are expected to show that you can work in major *and* minor keys of up to four sharps or flats.

Other aspects of the music that you might be asked to identify or explain include variation techniques (see page 45), inessential notes (see pages 25 and 134) and ornamentation. For example, the sign for an ornament might be omitted and you could be asked to write it in the correct position on the score, or to give its name and describe what it does (but you will not be asked to notate in full). Here are three common types of ornament that you may encounter:

- A **trill** (***tr***) consists of a rapid alternation between the printed note and the note above.
- A **turn** (∾) starts on the note above the printed note, followed by the printed note itself, then the note below it, and finally the printed note once more.
- An **acciaccatura** (pronounced *at-chak-ka-toora*) is a note printed in small type with a slash through its tail (♪). It is played as quickly as possible, either on or just before the beat, according to the context.

Exercise 12

Mozart, Clarinet Concerto, third movement

1. In bars 36–37, draw circles around all of the harmony notes in the clarinet part.
2. Which of the other clarinet quavers in these bars is an appoggiatura (see page 134) and which are passing notes?
3. Which of these quavers is *not* diatonic?

Instruments and textures

Throughout the AS course, techniques for combining instruments will keep coming under the spotlight and you should expect one or two questions about this aspect of the music in these extracts. As well as identifying instruments you should be prepared to recognise common performing techniques like glissando, pizzicato and the use of a mute.

Make sure you can tell the difference between instruments that may sound similar, such as horns and trombones, and saxophones and bassoons in their upper register.

You may well be asked to identify the **texture** of a passage. Some terms used for this are explained on page 136, but if you are asked to *describe* the texture it is important to give as much detail as you can: explain if parts are in unison or doubled an octave above or below, identify the instruments and explain exactly who is doing what. If the texture is imitative, be specific – say which instrument begins, which comes in next, what the pitch interval between these two entries is, and so on.

Exercise 13

Describe the texture in the following passage from the last movement of Mozart's Clarinet Concerto (it makes use of the theme already discussed on page 44). Compare your answer with ours on page 58.

Variation techniques

Whether the passages in the extract you have chosen are described as variations or not, they will certainly be closely related to one another, just as the passage *above* is related to the opening theme of the movement. You will be asked to identify the techniques that have been used to vary the original theme. This might be through change of key, tempo or harmony, different melodic decoration, changes in instrumentation and texture, or a combination of such features.

The use of variation techniques is not confined to the 18th century – if you choose extract 1B you will find that similar questions are asked. Almost all music includes variation of previously heard material and the techniques used are still important to composers today – could this include you, in your work for Section B of the composing unit? And, of course, variation is one of the most significant ingredients in jazz improvisation.

If you decide to answer questions on the popular music extract (1B) remember that it could come from before or after the period of the set jazz recordings that you will be studying (which come from the years 1920–1960). The style of the music may or may not be influenced by jazz. However, the type of question will be similar to those for extract 1A. There may be clear use of variation techniques but the extract may be from film music in which the original theme is altered significantly or reduced to one or two motifs for dramatic reasons.

Section B

Extract 2

There will be three tracks on your CD for this section of the paper. The first two of these will contain *different performances* of an extract from one of the three set orchestral works. They will be labelled 'Extract 2A' and 'Extract 2B' on the question paper. You may not bring copies of the scores into the examination room but you will be given a full score of the extract in the insert booklet (note that this score will *not* include CD timings).

The first few questions are usually about the **notation** of the score, such as the meaning of abbreviations or signs. You could be asked to transpose a clarinet or trumpet part into sounding pitch, or to write out on a treble or bass stave a viola phrase that is printed in the C clef. These are questions that you need to practise during the course – don't leave these skills until the night before the exam, especially since they are also likely to be needed when answering other types of questions.

There may well be one or two questions about **tonality** and tonal devices in this extract – a chord, a cadence, modulations and key relationships, sequences and pedal notes can all crop up. Recognising these in an orchestral score also needs practice.

You may be asked to describe the **texture** of the extract, to compare the passage with an earlier or later statement of the same theme (for which you will have to rely on your memory!), or to comment on how typical it is of this composer. Keep 'compare' questions in your mind as you study each score: notice when the woodwind are silent and when they play, whether they double the strings or have independent parts, what the difference is between the brass contributing a melody and simply filling out a chord, or how Bach's scoring for oboes differs from Schubert's.

You will be expected to be able to locate the extract within the movement as a whole. To do this, you must know the outline

structure of the movement and be able to recognise typical features of each section within it. You might be asked, for instance, whether an extract containing the second subject is from the exposition or the recapitulation (the clue usually lies in the key). Or, you might be asked to describe significant features of the music that comes before or after the actual extract.

The two recordings of the extract will have been chosen because they sound different in some ways. They may feature different **interpretations** of matters such as the tempo, dynamics, phrasing and articulation. The orchestras themselves may not be made up the same way. One of the excerpts might have been recorded by a large orchestra of modern instruments while the other was recorded by a much smaller ensemble of 'period' instruments, with relatively few string players to each part. The latter type of performance might also be at a lower pitch than its modern equivalent, reflecting the fact that pitch in the period 1700–1830 was somewhat lower than is customary today.

'Period' instruments are usually modern reconstructions that allow the performer to recreate the type of sound that might have been heard when early music was first performed.

Research into how music was performed in the past has also made it possible to use performing techniques that produce sounds more like the ones that the original composers would have expected to hear. This approach to performing music of the past is often referred to as **authentic** because it is said to be more faithful to the composer's intentions. Another view is that the music will sound different on modern instruments, but not necessarily worse, and that the composers of the past might well have welcomed the different sound.

Try to hear more than one type of recorded performance of each of your orchestral set works: all of them have been recorded many times during the last 50 years and historical research into styles of playing has influenced many of the more recent conductors.

You will not be asked to make a judgement about which of the performances is 'better', but you do need to understand some of the issues that will have influenced the two conductors in reaching their interpretative decisions.

Study the section on 'The score' in the next chapter (page 60) and work through all the exercises in it. This will give you the information and basic techniques needed to get started. Then tackle one of the three orchestral set works (you are advised to leave the Schubert till last). Listen with the score to more than one recording if at all possible. The more often you do this, the more easily you will be able to make musical sense of the score for yourself. Then, when the *sound* of each piece has begun to take root inside your head, study the relevant section in the chapter on the orchestral set works. Use your reading to inform your hearing – not the other way round. Don't treat the recordings as 'add-ons' to the information you read.

Extract 3

The third extract will be from one of the three set jazz recordings (see the list on page 59). There will be no score, so the questions will usually be about things that you can hear clearly on the recording.

There will be questions about the instruments and how they are used. You may be asked to describe the texture of a particular passage. Your answer should show that you understand the role of each instrument, whether frontline or rhythm section, and you should be prepared to describe particular features of the music that each plays, including any special effects such as glissando or the use of a harmon mute. You should also be able to recognise compositional devices used in the music, such as call-and-response, secondary rag or collective improvisation.

You may be asked to relate the extract to an earlier part of the piece that is not heard on the recording. You will need to remember the outline structure of the whole work and know it well enough to recognise exactly where the recorded extract comes in it. You will be expected to be able to describe the music that follows the extract, so you will need to be sure of the order of solo and chorus sections and be able to describe their main features.

You should know the names of the main performers in the band, particularly those who make a significant contribution to the music, including soloists and the rhythm section.

Section C

The last question in the examination will be an essay on one or more of the set works. Further details and practice questions are given in the Section C questions chapter of this book, starting on page 130.

Specimen answer for Exercise 13

The following answer doesn't include every possible point but it includes more than enough relevant detail for an excellent mark. The first point is the most important, but it needs to be supported by several specific examples, as shown.

The passage consists of a three-part texture in which the instruments change places in an increasingly contrapuntal way:

- In bar 1 the violins play the theme in 3rds, accompanied by a single harmony note
- In bar 2 the violas harmonise the first chord of the cadence by filling in the interval from A to D with ascending chromatic quavers
- These bars are then repeated a 3rd lower, but this time with clarinet and first violin in 3rds, and the second violins providing the chromatic bass line
- In bars 5–6 the violins again play the theme in 3rds (a 3rd lower still) and the clarinet takes over the chromatic accompaniment
- In bars 7–8 the violins play the theme in imitation while the clarinet provides a new, smooth bass line that descends low into its chalumeau register.

Set works

For Sections B and C of the paper you have to study six set works (described by OCR as the 'prescribed repertoire') – three orchestral scores from the 18th and early 19th centuries, plus three jazz recordings, from the period 1920–1960.

It is very important to check carefully that you are studying the right combination of pieces for the year and session in which you are going to take the exam:

	June 2009, January 2010, June 2010 and January 2011
Orchestral scores	1. J. S. Bach: Orchestral Suite No. 3 in D, BWV 1068 (Overture, Air and Gigue) 2. Mozart: Concerto in A for Clarinet and Orchestra, K. 622 (third movement) 3. Schubert: Symphony No. 8 in B minor, D. 759, 'Unfinished' (first movement)
Jazz recordings	1. Jelly Roll Morton: *Black Bottom Stomp* (1926) from *Jelly Roll Morton, Chicago Days, 1926–27*, Jazz Archives 158192 2. Count Basie: *Jumpin' at the Woodside* (1938) from *One O'Clock Jump (1936–39)*, Naxos Jazz Legends 8.120662 3. Miles Davis: *So What* from *Kind of Blue* (1959), Sony Jazz CK64935
	June 2011 and January 2012
Orchestral scores	1. J. S. Bach: Ouverture No. 3 in D, BWV 1068 (Overture, Air and Gigue) 2. Mozart: Concerto in A for Clarinet and Orchestra, K. 622 (third movement) 3. Schubert: Symphony No. 8 in B minor, D. 759, *Unfinished* (first movement)
Jazz recordings	1. Louis Armstrong and His Hot Five: *Alligator Crawl* (1927) from *Louis Armstrong 25 Greatest Hot Fives and Sevens*, Living Era AJA 5171 2. Charlie Parker: *Ko-Ko* (1945) from *Ornithology: Classic Recordings, 1945–1947*, Naxos Jazz Legends 8.120571 3. Gil Evans/Miles Davis: *It Ain't Necessarily So* from *Porgy and Bess* (1958), Sony Jazz CK65141

Note that any edition and any recording of the orchestral scores may be used but you *must* make sure that the jazz recordings you study are *exactly* the ones listed above.

Orchestral scores

Before starting on the set works, we first need to look at some of the conventions used in notating and interpreting orchestral scores.

The score

By convention, bars are numbered from the first *complete* bar onwards and superscript numerals are used for beats, so bar 8^1 means the first beat of bar 8.

The insert accompanying the exam paper will include a score of an extract from one of the orchestral set works that features in Section B. It won't look exactly the same as the copy that you have been using during your course but it will use the standard conventions and format found in most modern editions. Bars will be numbered from the beginning of the extract, so are unlikely to coincide with the bar numbering of the complete piece.

The scores you use in class will probably be miniature, pocket or study editions. Modern conductors use much larger full scores that let them read the notes more easily while standing. Scores of orchestral music were rarely published in printed form before the 19th century. In the early and mid 18th century, performances were usually directed from the harpsichord, often by the composer himself. If the composer was also the soloist in a concerto the solo part could be incomplete, the remainder being improvised on the night. The performance was often a very last-minute affair – it is no exaggeration to say that the ink on the page was sometimes still wet! The score was the master document from which a copyist rushed to prepare individual parts for the performers.

A virtuoso is a performer of great technical skill. Music which requires a high level of technical skill is sometimes called virtuosic.

During the 19th century access to music grew considerably. It was no longer the preserve of a privileged elite. A growing prosperous and educated middle class attended concerts and eagerly bought the latest music as soon as it was published. A public market for printed scores developed, sometimes copied and published without the composer's permission. The reputation of a work could spread widely, far beyond the big cities where there were opportunities to hear it performed, and people began to want to get to know fashionable pieces, not just hear them once only. Sometimes the first opportunity to hear a work would be in an arrangement for piano given by a touring virtuoso. Playing piano-duet versions of symphonies and overtures at home was a popular way of getting to know the classics of the orchestral repertoire in the late 19th and early 20th centuries.

With the advent of recording and broadcasting, and the growth of international tours, opportunities to hear and rehear orchestral music in different interpretations increased, and with these came a demand for cheaply-printed, pocket-sized scores for study purposes. Audiences began to be knowledgeable and critical about *how* music was performed. They could compare different approaches of conductors and performers, who often consciously tried to impose their own personal stamp on the music.

In the second half of the 20th century performers and scholars everywhere became concerned to ensure that the scores used in the preparation of performances reproduced what the composer had originally written more reliably – in other words, that they were authentic. Editors sought out manuscripts and the earliest printed editions, comparing them and trying to resolve problems or discrepancies between them in the light of what they knew about the conventions of the composer's time – in other words, performance practice. The result of such careful scholarship is often the publication of what is called an *Urtext* (original text) edition, which usually includes a detailed account of how the different sources have been used. Critical scores have also become common; these give a great deal more background information about the genesis of the music, and if the composer left any sketches of the work these might be included as well.

OCR does not require you to use any particular edition or recording of the orchestral scores. Depending on what your school or college has in its collection you may be working from a recent *Urtext* or from a much earlier, edited score. You should be aware that there might be differences, and some of the detail in the extract used in the exam might not be identical to the score you have been using. However, it is not necessary to study more than one edition of any of the orchestral set works. We have pointed out any significant differences between the main editions of the scores concerned.

Performance practices

In the mid-20th century the critical attitude and desire to recapture the original sound of the music extended to debate about how it should be performed. Musicians and audiences began to want performances that reflected more faithfully the type of sounds that original audiences might have heard. A great deal of research has been conducted into old instruments, performing techniques and the conventions of different periods and styles. Views differ on how far we should go in trying to reproduce exactly the techniques and sounds of the past. Having got used to hearing large orchestras, some people find the sound of the much smaller forces commonly used in the 18th century rather thin. However, textures tend to be much clearer and interesting new timbres emerge. Even performances on 'period' instruments usually differ from each other in tempo, dynamics, articulation, balance and so forth. Some of these differences could be the focus of the two recordings of the extract used in the exam.

Reading scores

Most modern scores use a standard format that may be different from the original layout used by the composer. Instruments are grouped into sections – woodwind at the top, followed by horns, then any other brass and percussion, and finally strings at the bottom. Staves within the woodwind and string sections are printed in order of pitch – highest at the top, lowest at the bottom. If there is a solo instrument (as in your Mozart concerto), its part is usually shown immediately above the strings, so that it is positioned next to the important first-violin stave.

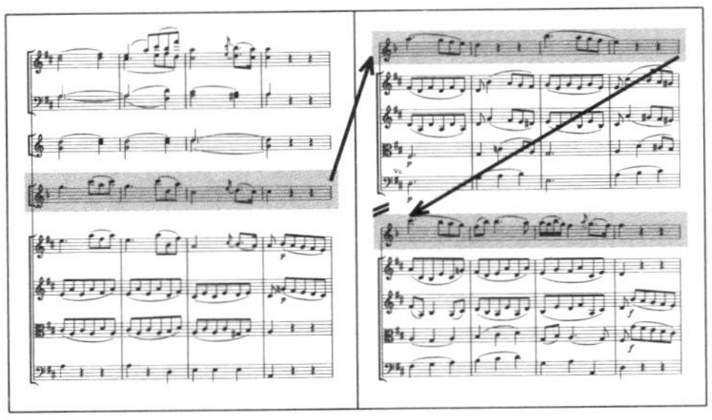

Most people find it easiest to read the first violin part (or the solo part in a concerto) when following a score, letting their eyes alight on the other staves when something interesting is happening in another section of the orchestra. Note that staves are sometimes omitted from scores when instruments are resting, since this allows more than one system (line of music) to fit on a page – for instance, the example *left* consists of three systems. This can make a score a little tricky to follow, but it saves paper and reduces the number of page turns. Systems are sometimes separated by a // sign.

Instrument names are often in Italian, but most are easily recognisable (such as *flauto*, a flute). However, be careful not to mistake *trombe* (trumpets) for trombones.

Oboes and bassoons (*fagotti*) were the original staples of the woodwind section, with the flute making an occasional appearance. Clarinets only regularly joined the orchestra towards the end of the 18th century (they were not used by Bach). By about 1800 the woodwind were usually scored in pairs (two flutes, two oboes, two clarinets and two bassoons) – a layout known as **double woodwind**.

Horns were also usually used in pairs in the 18th century and are always placed above the trumpets in the score, reflecting the fact that they are often used to blend with the woodwind. Trombones had been used in opera orchestras in the late 18th century but only began to feature regularly in orchestral music after 1800, usually in threes.

In some editions of the Schubert the letter names for the timpani notes are in German: H (= B) and Fis (= F♯).

Throughout the 18th century, the percussion normally consisted of just a pair of timpani played by one person. The notes to which they are to be tuned are given at the beginning of the score and are usually the tonic and dominant of the main key (D and A in the Bach, B and F♯ in the Schubert).

Cellos and double basses usually play the same notes, although the basses actually sound an octave lower. Because the lowest string on the cello is C below the bass stave, while on a standard double bass it is E, composers sometimes wrote independent bass parts when the cello line went too low for the basses to follow. They also occasionally used just the cellos for special effect, as in bars 150–153[1] of the last movement of Mozart's Clarinet Concerto.

If a pair of wind instruments has only a single line of music then both are expected to play – unless it is marked *solo* to show that only the first instrument is required. The direction *a 2* (*zu* 2 in German) will appear if they are then to resume playing in unison. The figures 1. and 2., or the use of upward or downward stems on the notes, also indicate which instrument is to play:

Schubert, Symphony No. 8 in B minor, first movement

Scores did not specify how many string players were required – it depended on factors such as the number of wind parts, size of the venue, what could be afforded and availability of players. The author of the *Musikalisches Lexicon* (musical dictionary), published in 1802, recommended six first violins, six second violins, four violas, four cellos and three double basses for symphonies – 23 string players in total – although both smaller and larger string sections than this were used during the 18th century, depending on circumstances. In comparison, a modern symphony orchestra is likely to have around 60 string players.

You need to develop an ability to 'hear' internally, the sounds that the score suggests – not just the melodic lines, but the rhythms and harmonies, the timbres of individual instruments, and the effects of combining them in different types of texture. This will become easier after studying and repeatedly listening to the music.

Clefs

As well as treble and bass clefs you will need to learn to find your way around the **C clef** (𝄡). This is used for several mid-range instruments which would otherwise need a lot of leger lines if notated using either treble or bass clefs.

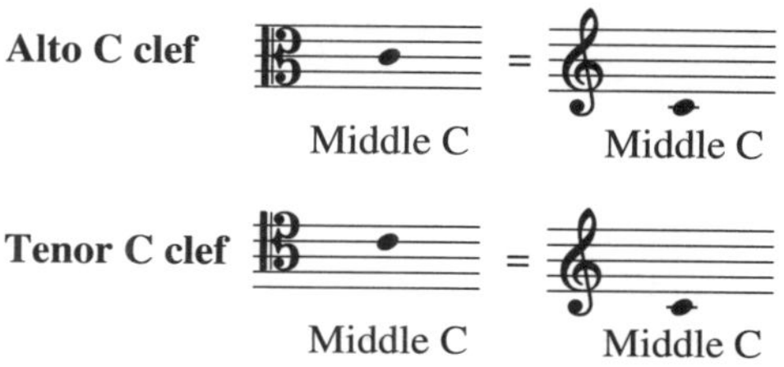

Wherever the C clef is placed on a stave, the stave-line through its centre fixes the position of middle C, as shown *right*. The alto C clef straddles the middle line of the stave and is used for viola parts, while the tenor C clef is one line higher and is used for notes in the upper registers of the bassoon, trombone and cello:

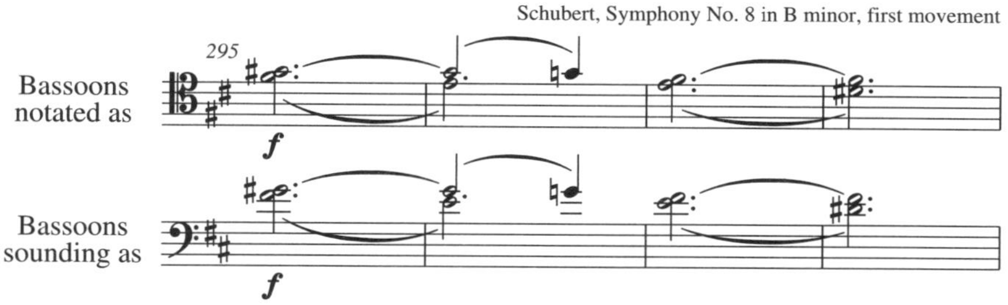

Your score of Schubert's Symphony No. 8 in B minor may use either the alto C clef or the tenor C clef for the upper trombone parts, depending on which edition you have.

Exercise 14

If you are asked to rewrite a C-clef passage into either the treble or bass clef, use middle C as a reference point and check every few notes that you haven't slipped in pitch as you go. When you are asked to write out a part in a different clef always remember to put the correct key signature at the beginning of the stave.

1. Write out the following viola part on a sheet of manuscript paper, using the treble clef.

2. Write out the following bassoon parts twice: (i) using the bass clef (you will have to use quite a large number of leger lines for this) and (ii) using the treble clef:

Schubert, Symphony No. 8 in B minor, first movement

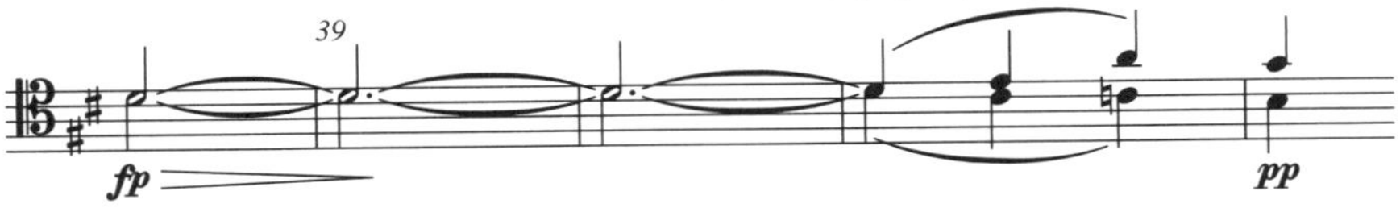

Transposing instruments

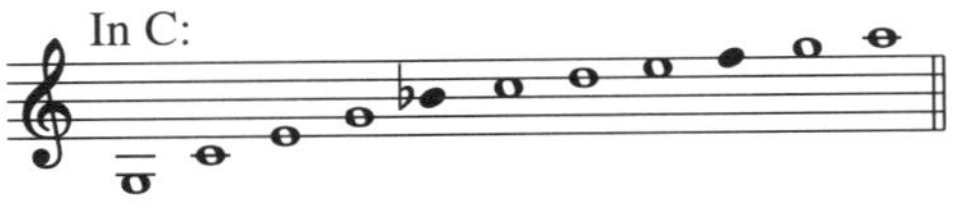

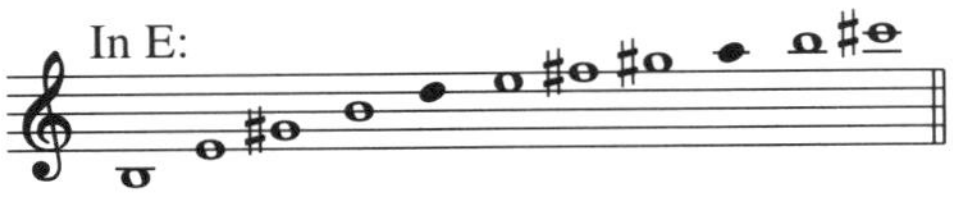

Modern horns and trumpets can play a wide range of chromatic notes, using valves developed during the 19th century. However, only **natural trumpets** and **natural horns** (i.e. instruments without valves) were available to Bach, Mozart and Schubert. These were limited to a set of pitches determined by the total length of tube in the instrument. For example, if the composer specified a trumpet in C, the notes shown *left* would be available (those in black tending to sound a little out of tune). Horns used a similar series of pitches an octave lower, although they were sometimes required to reach higher or lower notes.

To obtain a different series of pitches – say, for a piece in D major – the length of the total tube could be changed, using a removable piece of coiled tubing called a crook. A trumpet crooked in D would produce the series of pitches shown *left*.

Once the crook is in place, there is no significant difference for the player between the examples shown *left*. If you play the top stave while crooked in D, it will sound like the second stave. Play it again while crooked in E and it will sound like the third stave shown *left*. It was therefore more helpful to players to write trumpet and horn parts in C, leaving the crook to ensure that the notes were transposed (changed in pitch) to the required key. Key signatures were thus not usually needed for horn or trumpet parts at this time, although composers had to specify the pitch of the crook to use (e.g. 'in D'). This was usually the tonic key of the movement and if the music modulated the instrument would either have to be left out or be restricted to whatever pitches would fit the new key.

In order to read a score accurately you need to know which parts are written for transposing instruments and what key each of those instruments is in:

J. S. Bach, Orchestral Suite No. 3 in D, Overture

Schubert, Symphony No. 8 in B minor, first movement

Mozart, Clarinet Concerto, third movement

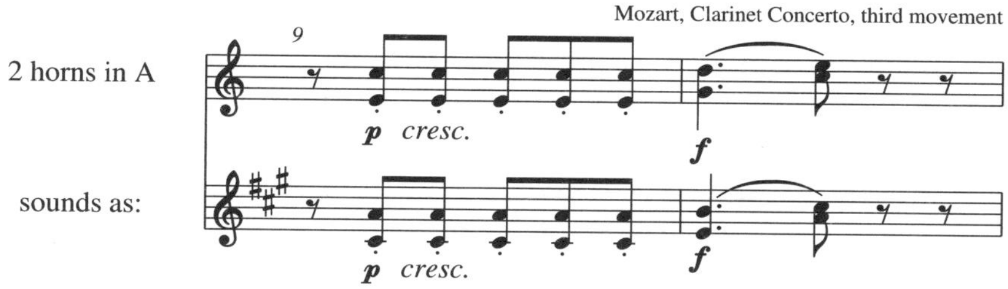

Schubert, Symphony No. 8 in B minor, first movement

You will see from these four examples that:

- Trumpets in D sound a major 2nd higher than written
- Trumpets in E sound a major 3rd higher than written
- Horns in A sound a minor 3rd lower than written
- Horns in D sound a minor 7th lower than written.

The description of the instrument tells you the note that sounds when C is played. For example, a trumpet in D sounds D when C is played. From this you can deduce that *all* of its notes sound a tone higher than written.

There are a few modern editions that show transposing instruments at their sounding pitch – for example, the Bärenreiter score of the Bach suite prints the trumpet parts at sounding pitch. However, the exam extract is likely to show what the composer wrote, so you must understand the principle of transposing and learn to interpret this notation.

Clarinets are also notated as transposing instruments but with an appropriate key signature. This is because early clarinets were designed so that the fingering in the upper register corresponded with that of the oboe, the principal woodwind instrument of the time. Because the clarinet is a slightly longer instrument, the actual notes sounded were a bit lower than those on the oboe. Makers stamped the clarinet with the name of the note that would sound when C was fingered – the most common types being B♭ and A.

The B♭ clarinet sounds a tone lower than the written notes, because B♭ is a tone lower than C. The A clarinet sounds a minor 3rd lower than written, because A is a minor 3rd lower than C. Which of the two instruments to use depends on the overall key of the music (experienced clarinettists today have both B♭ and A instruments). Mozart's Clarinet Concerto and Schubert's *Unfinished* Symphony both use clarinets in A.

The information given in the preceding pages provides most of what you need to know to get started on the mechanics of score-reading. You need to understand clefs and transposing instruments in order to read the notation accurately. Being able to do this is particularly vital when it comes to answering questions about keys, chords and cadences.

Even if you don't encounter a direct question about keys, when you are asked to identify where in the movement the extract comes from, the best clue often lies in its key.

Interpretation

Getting the notes right is the first priority for an orchestra but there's more to a satisfactory performance than just that. How the notes are played is important. Most composers will have given some guidance about this in their scores.

Tempo

Few tempo indications were given in Baroque music – performers were expected to know how fast a movement should go from its style and context. In the absence of any instructions in Baroque

Some editors add tempo markings for the benefit of modern performers, such as the French expression *'Grave'* at the beginning of Bach's Orchestral Suite in D in some scores. However, Bach's only tempo instruction in the entire suite is *'viste'* (an old spelling for the modern French word *'vite'*, meaning 'quick') at bar 24.

music, the clues in the time signature may be important, not only for the speed but also for how the beats should be weighted. For instance, at bar 24 in Bach's Overture, the time signature changes from four crotchet beats per bar to two minim beats, suggesting that the rhythm should have a lively bounce (and thus stopping the quavers of the countersubject from sounding pedestrian). In the Air, a performance that gives too much prominence to the quavers in the bass may risk sounding as though there are eight beats in a bar, rather than the four of the time-signature. Baroque performers would know from experience how fast dances such as the Gigue should be played, but we cannot be certain of precise speeds until composers started to use metronome markings in the 19th century – and even these were not always accurate at first.

It is rare to hear a performance of any long movement from the 18th or early 19th century in which the tempo is exactly the same all the way through. When you compare recordings of interpretations of Bach's Suite, listen to the endings of movements – is there a grand slowing down (in a rather 'Romantic' manner), or just a slight slackening of speed (a more modern 'authentic' approach)? The last movement of Mozart's Clarinet Concerto has such a strong sense of forward drive that conductors will usually not want to let it sag anywhere, but the soloist may want a little more scope for expressive playing, for instance at the beginning of the F♯ minor theme (bar 137). In the 19th century the use of **rubato** (playing with rhythmic freedom for expressive effect) was common. Be prepared, therefore, for performances of Schubert's *Unfinished* Symphony to have quite a bit of push-and-pull in them.

Dynamics

Again, in Baroque times musicians understood the conventional practices of their day and so very few dynamic markings were written into their parts. In some editions of Bach's Overture the letter ***p*** has been added to indicate passages of accompaniment. The resulting abrupt contrasts of ***f*** and ***p***, without any crescendo or diminuendo between them, are often referred to as **terraced dynamics**. This doesn't mean that individual phrases were played in a dead-pan way: musicians were expected to be able to play a slow, lyrical melody in the way that it might be sung, with a sense of breathing and flexibility. In the Air, for instance, you will probably notice that most orchestras colour the first, long F♯ with some sort of crescendo.

Mozart also makes strong contrasts between his solo passages and **tutti** sections (*tutti* means 'all' and refers to passages in which everyone plays). But, by this time, the expressive effect of an entire orchestra making a well-drilled crescendo was also appreciated. The soloist's opening repeated staccato quavers, which turn out to be a pervading feature of the movement, are immediately taken up by the orchestra with a crescendo from ***p*** to ***f*** (bars 9–10).

Schubert is generous with dynamic markings: his strong imaginative sense brings home what the word 'dynamic' really means – force and movement. In the first movement of his *Unfinished* Symphony the music is always *moving* forward (even when there is silence, as in bar 62), and Schubert is careful to indicate the degree of *force* to be used, with the frequent appearance of ***fz***, ***ffz*** and even ***fp*** (bar 29^2) – what do you think this means? Again, such signs do not have absolute meanings – they are relative and every performance will therefore be different. One conductor's range of volume from ***pp*** to ***ff*** will differ from another's.

Articulation

Articulation refers to the way in which notes are played – whether they are to be run together (legato), detached (staccato), accented (marcato) or held firmly (tenuto). Again, such markings are only indications and don't tell performers precisely how long to hold a note, or exactly how much pressure to apply. They will all do these things slightly differently.

Slurs mean different things to different kinds of instrumentalists: to wind players they give clues as to how to tongue notes, to string players they offer ideas on how to bow the notes.

But a composer's intentions are often not completely clear. The various sources for Bach's Orchestral Suite in D differ slightly in some places, and there are even inconsistencies within a movement. If you have access to the latest Eulenburg score of Bach's Suite, compare bars 42–58 in the Overture with the version in Appendix A, and bars 71–89 with the version in Appendix B. There are many small differences in the way the passages are slurred but there is also a difference within the alternative versions between passages that are very similar.

Other terms and symbols

You also need to understand the following terms, which all apply to string instruments:

- **Pizzicato** (pluck the strings) and **arco** (bow the strings).
- **Double stopping** (playing two notes on adjacent strings at the same time) – limited combinations of three- and even four-part chords are also possible (see *right*)
- Bowed **tremolo** (rapid repetitions of a single note produced by alternate up and down bows). This busy and excited effect is indicated by beams through the stem of the note concerned, the number of beams indicating the speed of the repetitions, as shown *right*.

Schubert, Symphony No. 8 in B minor
first movement

Notice that Schubert also uses tremolo to indicate timpani rolls, but Bach uses the trill sign (***tr***) for this.

Comparing interpretations

In the exam, some of the differences between the interpretations of extract 2 may be obvious, such as tempo and dynamics, while others, such as the balance between instruments, are likely to be more subtle. Look closely at the expressive details in the score, particularly articulation marks, slurring and phrasing.

Following scores

Orchestral scores contain a great deal of information and to begin with you may want to concentrate on keeping up with the music, probably by following the melody, whichever part it is in. As you become more familiar with the sound, and how it relates to the layout, practise trying to hear how different instruments perform different roles in the texture. For example, can you hear:

- When the flute doubles the first violins an octave above, for instance in your Mozart score, bars 77–81?
- When the horn plays a pedal in the middle of the texture, for instance in your Schubert score, bars 53–59?
- Which instrument supplies the bass note, for instance in your Schubert score bars 353–355; or the third of the chord, for instance in the last chord of Bach's Overture?
- How a timpani note fits the harmony, for instance in your Schubert score bar 249? (It is the seventh of $C\sharp^7$.)

Get into the habit of noticing the effect of different timbres, how various combinations of instruments are used, and how a composer can create a crescendo by piling on the instruments rather than just increasing the dynamic levels.

As you listen, sometimes focus on details, sometimes listen to the whole: your eye on the score can identify techniques and effects which your ear may only be dimly aware of at first.

From time to time you may notice something that strikes you as an effective technique or combination of instruments that might be adapted for use in your own compositions. You could begin by experimenting with the variety of expressive sounds that can be obtained by different sorts of doubling.

BWV 1068 is the number of this work in the standard catalogue of Bach's music compiled in the 20th century. You may see this suite described as an Ouverture, a title borrowed from that of its substantial opening movement.

If you don't already have a score and CD of this work, the Eulenburg Audio + Score edition (EAS 114) offers a clear, modern score, packaged with a recording, at a competitive price (and which also includes Bach's Orchestral Suite No. 4).

St Thomas School, Leipzig, photographed before its demolition in 1902. Bach worked in this building and lived in rooms on the lower-left side.

Bach: Orchestral Suite No. 3 in D, BWV 1068

There is no autograph score of this work. Modern editions are based on a variety of sources that include a set of parts, some in Bach's own handwriting, some in that of his second surviving son, C. P. E. Bach, as well as on a score and parts copied from manuscripts by a Leipzig student not long after Bach's death. The prefaces to the Bärenreiter and Eulenburg editions of the score explain these sources in more detail.

Like many composers of his day, Bach frequently reused music, remodelling it to suit the availability and abilities of different performers. It was quite common, therefore, for there to be more than one version of a work. Bach's duties involved the weekly composition, rehearsal and performance of large quantities of new music and it is hardly surprising, under such pressure, that he adapted earlier pieces. Some musicologists suggest that this work may have been intended originally for strings (and continuo) only, and that the oboes, trumpets and drums were added for a later performance, but no one knows for certain.

Johann Sebastian Bach (1685–1750) came from a north-German family that had a long history of producing musicians. During the period spanning the 16th to the 19th centuries more than 70 members of the family were active as organists, choirmasters and composers. His own sons continued in this tradition. In 1723 Bach left his job at the court in Cöthen, where he had opportunities to compose much instrumental music, to become Director of Music at St Thomas's Church in Leipzig, an important city appointment. He was not everyone's first choice – other composers had been head-hunted but refused the job – and he experienced constant, niggling, political difficulties. The workload was considerable as it included composing and preparing for performance considerable quantities of new music for the main services on Sundays and church festivals.

J. S. Bach also composed much educational music for his family and pupils, such as the Inventions and the *Notebook for Anna Magdalena Bach* – both of which piano teachers still use today. In 1729 Bach also took on responsibility for the Collegium Musicum, an orchestra of up to 40 players, mainly students and amateurs.

The origins of the Orchestral Suite No. 3 in D are not known with any certainty. It may have been arranged from earlier music that Bach had written in Cöthen, but it is likely that the first performance of the work in its current form was given by the *Collegium Musicum* in 1729; it was played again in 1731.

The suite

As a young man Bach had shown a lively interest in most types of contemporary music and was thoroughly familiar with the latest French and Italian styles, as well as that of the principal German composers of his day. Although he travelled when he could to hear leading performers, Bach mostly studied new music by copying it out and making arrangements of it. His own style is a synthesis of French, Italian and German techniques. This suite has mostly French characteristics.

The custom of composing dances to perform and listen to, rather than for dancing, and then issuing them in collections or 'suites' had grown steadily during the later years of the 17th century. Bach composed many suites for solo instruments and probably several more than the four orchestral ones that have survived.

Although the work is an orchestral suite, Bach didn't use this term himself. It is often described as an 'Ouverture', the title of its first movement. It is fairly obvious that this is the French word for overture, the opening piece in a longer work. But using this title for the whole of BWV 1068, as well as for its first movement, is potentially confusing, so we will refer to the complete work as a suite in the rest of this section.

Bach's Orchestral Suite No. 3 in D consists of five movements: **Overture**, **Air**, Gavotte, Bourrée and **Gigue**, of which you have to study the three printed in bold type. The gavotte, bourrée and gigue are all dance styles, while the famous air (which simply means a song) is a more reflective movement, although it uses the same structure as the dances.

Usually the pieces in a Baroque suite were all in the same key, although sometimes one was in the tonic minor for contrast. This consistency of tonality was normally the only link between them – there was rarely any sort of thematic link.

Each movement is self-contained and each of the dances explores a single idea. Indeed, one of the most striking differences between Baroque and Classical styles is that most Baroque music aims to develop a single mood (known in German as an *affekt*) while Classical music generally exploits the dramatic tension between contrasting ideas.

The orchestra

There was no standard format for an orchestra in the late Baroque period (roughly 1700–1750). They differed from princely court to princely court, from church to church and from one occasion to another. The two constant features, however, were:

- A small body of strings (violins, violas, cellos and either double basses or the rather older violone)
- One or more chordal instruments, such as a harpsichord, organ or lute.

The presence of a continuo group, most notably including a harpsichord, is one of the most identifiable features of Baroque ensemble music.

When you listen to a recording of the suite, check that you can hear a harpsichord – older 'Romantic' style interpretations may not include one since Bach's textures in this work are already quite full. Then focus on what the harpsichordist is playing: every recording will be different. The timbre of the instrument will also vary, as will the sense of whether it is in the foreground or the background, depending on where it was placed during the recording process and how the sounds have been edited.

The bass part was also used by the chordal instrument(s) as the basis for improvising harmonies to fill out the texture. This part was known as the **basso continuo** (continuous bass) and it would sometimes include numbers and other symbols to indicate the chords required, the result being known as a **figured bass**.

The process of **realising** the bass required skill – the performer was expected to play the harmonies in a way that reflected the rhythm and mood of the piece. And if, as was common, figures were omitted or incomplete, players were still expected to know what chords to improvise from the context of the bass line and the harmonic conventions of the day.

Baroque orchestras sometimes also included wind instruments – usually oboes, in which case bassoons might also be used, playing essentially the same bass part as the cellos and double basses. Trumpets and timpani were often added for music of a ceremonial character.

As so little is known about the first performance of this work, we cannot be sure about the details of the orchestra that Bach used, but it was probably quite large for its time. If there were only a few string players to each part the melodic line would have been in danger of being swamped by the trumpets and timpani – is this why two oboes double the first violin part in much of this music?

The timpani are tuned to D (tonic) and A (dominant) and their use is largely limited to *tutti* passages in the tonic or dominant keys – they usually drop out during modulations. The three trumpets are also in D. In Bach's day these parts would have been played on **natural trumpets** (see page 64) and so had to be limited to the available notes. Players tended to specialise in a particular part of the available range. It was only at the very top that the pitches were close enough together to play melodies, and this was known as the **clarino** register (see the margin note on page 41 for a related use of the term clarino).

Exercise 15

Write out at sounding pitch the three trumpet parts in bars 22^6–24 of the Gigue. The first two notes of each part have been given. Do not use key signatures, but add all necessary accidentals.

In late-Baroque orchestral music it was common for the oboes to double the violins. Here, *both* oboes double the first violins in some passages (such as the opening of the Overture and throughout the Gigue), while at other times oboe 1 doubles the first violins and oboe 2 doubles the second violins (as in bars 24b–42 of the Overture). In some places, such as during the Air, the oboes are silent. In bars 50–56 of the Overture they sustain harmonies in the background of the texture, while in bars 76–80 of the same movement oboe 1 plays a simplified version of the first violin part while oboe 2 decorates the second violin part.

During the last 100 years, research into instrument construction and 18th-century performing techniques has made it possible to recreate the sounds of the period. Trumpets are not the only instruments that were different in Baroque times. Oboes had fingerholes (like a recorder) and only three keys. String instruments were of a lighter construction; the strings were under less tension than those of a modern instrument and they were all made of gut. Violins and violas were played without a chin- or shoulder-rest, and cellos did not have spikes. Bows also differed from their modern counterparts and were used in a different way. The overall string sound tended to be drier than it is today, often more detached, with less use of singing legato and with **vibrato** mainly reserved for use as a special effect.

Vibrato refers to a slight undulation in sound, often used for expressive effect on longer notes by string and wind players (and singers).

Research has also indicated that the overall pitch of music in the 18th century would have been about a semitone lower than concert pitch today.

Overture

The French word *ouverture* means an opening – a movement that serves as an introduction. This one is in the style of a French overture, commonly used at the start of an opera in Baroque France, but also adopted by German composers of the time such as Bach and Handel.

The two main elements in all French overtures are:

- A slow introduction featuring dotted rhythms, which is repeated
- A fast fugal section.

Bach rounds off the fast section with a highly varied repeat of the opening material, and then directs that the fast section (followed by the slow ending) should be repeated, resulting in the structure shown *right* for the entire movement.

	Bars		
𝄆	1–24a	Slow, dotted rhythms	𝄇
𝄆	24b–106	Fast, fugal	
	107–122	Slow, dotted rhythms	𝄇

Slow introduction

The overture, like each of the other movements in this suite, is in D major. The home key is established by means of **tonic pedals** in bars 1–3^2 and 4–6^1, separated by a dominant-7th chord (bar $3^{3–4}$). The music then moves to the dominant, A major, before passing briefly through E minor (bars 9–10) and B minor (bars 11–13).

Listen for a surprise at bar 13^1: Bach prepares our ears for a perfect cadence in B minor but substitutes the brighter-sounding chord of B *major*, with its major 3rd (D♯) prominent in the bass. This is a chromatic chord, not a modulation, and it eventually leads back to a strong cadence in A major in bars 17^3–18.

Bach then passes through G major (the subdominant key) in bars 19–20 before returning to the tonic (D) for the end of the slow introduction. It finishes with an imperfect cadence, ready for the music to either return to the start or to lead on to the fugue.

The harmonies of this first section are full of interesting details. Bach was skilful at using a wide range of devices – auxiliary notes, suspensions, pedals and sequences to enrich his harmonic palette. From the very first he sets up tension: the tonic pedal seems to want to stop the music moving forward, but the harmonies change over it, eventually becoming so dissonant that the piece seems almost forced to resolve onto dominant harmony in the second half of bar 3. The chords above the pedal are shown *left*. Listen to how dissonant the bass D sounds by bar 3^1. It is now hanging on as a suspension against A^7 above, this chord eventually forcing the dissonance to resolve to C♯ on bar 3^3.

Bar 1		2	3
D	Bm	Em^7	A^7 ———
I	vi	ii^7	V^7 ———
Pedal (D) ———			

Trumpets and drums are prominent in the fanfare-like opening. They drop out at bar 6 when the music starts to modulate and don't return until bar 18.

The entire 24 bars are dominated by dotted rhythms – the most characteristic feature of the first section of a French overture. It is generally accepted now that these would have been performed in a way that slightly lengthened the dotted quaver, making the semiquaver after it sound brisker, Although often referred to as 'double-dotting' or 'over-dotting', the pattern is usually articulated with a brief rest before the second note of each pair, as shown *left*.

Written

Performed

Exercise 16

Write a detailed commentary on the harmonies in bars 107–110 of the Overture.

The fugue

The distinctive feature of a fugue is its **contrapuntal**, intensely imitative, texture. Each part is treated as an equal and is referred to as a 'voice' even if the fugue is for instruments. This example is for four voices – essentially the string parts, since the oboes do little more than double violins and the trumpets mainly bolster the texture or shadow the violin parts.

The principal theme of a fugue is known as the **subject** and here it is announced by the first violins. This is immediately followed by the entry of the second violins with the same theme, but now transposed down a 5th. The transposed version of the subject is called the **answer**. While the second violins play the answer, the first violins continue with a new idea called the **counter-subject**:

The second-violin part can be described as a 'real answer' because it is an exact transposition of the subject – notice that this results in the G of the subject being answered as C♮. If one or more notes had been changed to keep the answer entirely within the tonic key, the result would be called a 'tonal answer'.

Bach creates a short link by repeating bar 26 in sequence to form bar 27, after which the viola comes in with the subject (bar 28), followed by the bass part with the answer in bar 29. Meanwhile, the upper parts continue with further counter-subjects that not only fit in counterpoint with the subject/answer but also with each other (see the diagram *below*).

This first section, with its alternation of subject and answer (until all the 'voices' have entered) is called the **exposition**. The following diagram summarises the order of entries and how the opening material continues to be extended in the exposition:

Bars	*24*	*25*	*26*	*27*	*28*	*29*	*30*
Violin 1	**Subject**	**Counter-subject 1**		**Sequence**	**Counter-subject 2**	**Counter-subject 3**	
Violin 2		**Answer**		**Sequence**	**Counter-subject 1**	**Counter-subject 2**	
Viola					**Subject**	**Counter-subject 1**	
Bass						**Answer**	

Exercise 17

Write out in the treble clef the viola part in bars 28–29³.

The fugue doesn't stop when all the parts have had a turn with the subject – the imitative texture continues, but any of the different melodic ideas that have been introduced in the exposition can be taken up, extended and played with. Because the parts might enter in a different order, the relationships between subject, answer and countersubjects will change. For instance, a part that started out at the bottom of the texture can be found later at the top or in the middle. Counterpoint that is composed so that the themes can be placed anywhere in the texture without sounding strained is called **invertible counterpoint**. Here is an example from bars 32³–35¹:

Because the many semiquavers result in long bars, references to beat numbers in this section are based on four crotchet beats per bar.

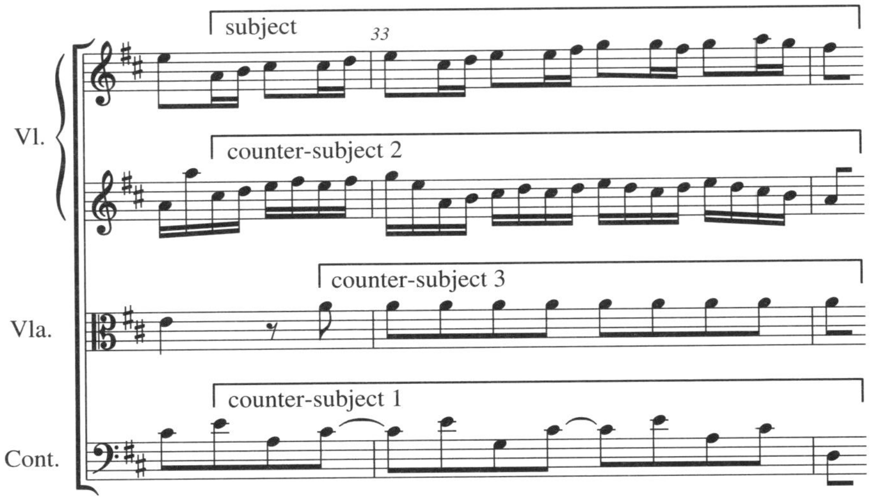

The rest of the fugue includes short passages in related keys, when the parts again state the subject and answer – these are known as middle entries. It ends with a set of final entries (bars 89–107) which are exactly the same as bars 24–42, but in a full texture.

An alternative source for this movement labels the first violin part in the episodes '*concertino*', a word implying that solo instruments may once have been used in these sections.

The passages of strict imitation alternate with freer ones, called **episodes**, in which the texture is usually lighter and a short motif from earlier is extended and varied in a process of 'continuous expansion'. An example of this is the development of counter-subject 2, which starts in bar 42. At bar 50 the subject starts to creep back in, initially played by the second violin in the relative minor key. Another such passage starts in bar 71.

We can now summarise the structure of the fugue as follows:

Exposition	Bars 24–31[1], extended to bar 42[1]
Episode 1	Bars 42[1]–58[1]
Middle entries	Bars 58[1]–71[1]
Episode 2	Bars 71[1]–89[1] (expanded)
Final entries	Bars 89[1]–107[1] (a repeat of the exposition's order of entries, but in a full texture from the start)

Final section

In bar 107 the final chord of the fugue seamlessly overlaps with the start of a shortened version of the slow introduction. It begins in a similar way to bar 1 but the opening theme now has a falling rather than a rising outline. Bach restates bars 20–21 almost exactly in bars 119–120, but elsewhere he tends to explore ideas from the introduction rather than repeating them exactly.

Exercise 18

1. Episode 2 begins in a similar way to Episode 1, but in a different key. Explain the relationship between these two keys.
2. Where in the middle entries is there a modulation to F♯ minor?

Binary form

Each of the remaining movements in the suite is in **binary form**, the most common structure for Baroque dances. It consists of two repeated sections, the first of which generally modulates to the dominant (if the key is major) while the second, longer section visits other related keys before returning to the tonic. Although this is often represented as ‖: A :‖: B :‖, the two sections are based on the same thematic material, maintaining the Baroque principle of a single *affekt* (mood) throughout the movement.

Air

The air is not a dance, although this example shares the binary form used for Baroque dances. Here it simply means a lyrical melody. Bach often introduced a contrasting movement of this sort among the dances in his suites.

The melody seems able to unfold forever, only coming to rest briefly in bar 6. The sense of forward movement comes from the 'walking bass', particularly during the long opening note of the melody. The bass makes its way steadily and purposefully towards the cadences and even propels the music back to the beginning with its only deviation from quaver movement – the semiquavers in bar 6.

Study the bass part in detail as it will help you to identify the harmonies, recognise keys and hear how the movement is based on two-bar phrases throughout. The octave leaps in the bass have been removed from the start of the following harmonic outline:

Exercise 19

Complete the bass part in bars 3–4 of the example *above*, omitting the octave leaps. Then comment on how bar 4 relates to bar 3.

Listen to the recording of the first four bars and focus on the chords rather than the bass part: can you *hear* how slowly the harmonies change? In bar 1 the chords (I and vi) occur on beats 1 and 3 – the bass note between acts as a very slow passing note. The G♯ in bar 2 is another passing note, this time chromatic, but it has the effect of transforming the harmony into a chord of E major – the dominant of A major, which is the next chord. But this is just a chromatic chord, not a modulation. It's too early in the piece to modulate and Bach cancels the G♯ immediately after the A-major chord to drive the music straight back towards the tonic.

The D♯s and C♮s in bar 3 are not just chromatic colouring – they *do* briefly turn the music towards E minor in bar 4. But Bach does not stay there – he uses the E-minor chord in bar 4 as a **pivot chord** (see page 33). What we initially hear as chord i of E minor, therefore turns out to be chord ii in the tonic key as the music unfolds. The first main modulation, to the dominant key of A major, follows in bars 5–6.

Identifying the harmonies in this passage is made more difficult by Bach's fondness for **suspensions** (see page 134) in the melodic lines. For example, the long F♯ at the start of the melody becomes a suspension on the first beat of bar 2, but its resolution to E on the second beat of that bar is delayed by semiquavers on B and G as well as by an appoggiatura on F♯. This can be described as a 'decorated resolution' of the suspension.

Exercise 20

Identify and explain: (i) an example of a suspension in the viola part in bars 1–4, and (ii) an example of a suspension in the second violin part in bars 4–6.

The Eulenburg miniature score (E.E.7022) includes an Appendix that shows extra ornamentation. If you have this edition, when you listen to a recording, try to identify which version is being played (or whether the performers are adding even more ornamentation).

The melody is highly decorated, not only by suspensions and ornaments such as those in bar 2, but by passing notes, accented passing notes and written-out appoggiaturas, such as the E in bar 3^4. If you have a clear concept of the underlying harmonies, you will find such melodic features much easier to spot.

Bars 1–6 have been discussed in detail and you should now be able to apply the same approach to the rest of the Air for yourself. Start with the bass, working in two-bar phrases. Particular points to notice are:

- Bar 7 starts in A but the G(♮) in the bass on the second beat of the bar immediately counters this, while bar 8 contains another passing reference to E minor
- Bars 9–10 come to rest in B minor, the relative minor
- Bars 11–12 return to the dominant (A major) but G♮ on the last beat of bar 12 turns the chord of A into the dominant 7th (V^7d) of the original tonic key
- Bars 13–14 form a rising sequence (the chords are outlined *left*) over a chromatically ascending bass, increasing the tension and countering the mainly downward movement heard so far

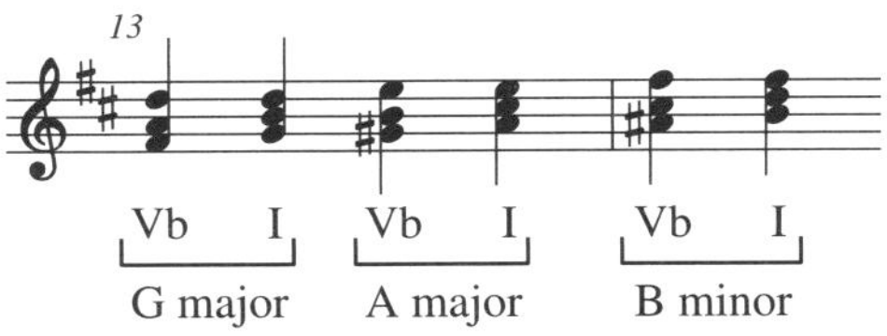

- Bars 15–18 include a passing reference to the subdominant key (G major) – a typical Bachian harmonic move just before the final cadence in the tonic key.

You can learn a great deal that could be of use in your own harmony exercises from Bach's handling of harmonies and use of decorative melodic techniques in this movement. Closely studying a short passage like this can also help you to answer the questions on unfamiliar extracts in Section A of the listening paper.

Exercise 21

Listen to two different performances of the Air. What differences, if any, do you hear in the use and treatment of ornamentation in the first-violin part?

Gigue

Gigue is French for jig – a lively dance in compound time. Like most Baroque dances, it is usually in binary form, and it generally formed the last movement of a suite.

This Gigue is typical of the style in its use of regular (four-bar) phrase lengths and in its largely homophonic texture. As so often happens in binary dances, the second section is much longer than the first. In this case the 72 bars divide into three groups, each 24 bars in length: 𝄆 0^6–24^5 𝄇𝄆 24^6–48^5 48^6–72^5 𝄇.

Because bar 1 is always the first *complete* bar in a passage, any notes before this are described as being in 'bar 0'.

The best way to get to know this movement is to work through it in four-bar phrases (remember that they all begin with an anacrusis on the last quaver of a bar). Then compare the starts and ends of the three sections. The match between their dotted-crotchet openings is easy to spot but the similarity of the endings of the first and last sections is concealed by a passage of invertible counterpoint: compare the melody of bars 19–24 (oboes doubling first violins) with the basso continuo part in bars 66–72, and vice versa. But the first passage is six bars long, the other is seven – where does Bach stretch the second one? He makes the chromatic sequence of bars 19–20 last an extra bar (bar 68). Why did he do that? To get back to the tonic key (D major).

Practice test

In your score of the Gigue, study the passage from bar 48^6 to the end and answer the following questions:

1. Explain the sign ***tr*** above the timpani part in bar 49.
2. Write out in the treble clef the viola part in bars 53–55.
3. Write out at sounding pitch the part played by trumpet 2 in bars 63–65.
4. Identify the key and cadence in bars 51–52.
5. To what key does the music modulate in bars 54–56?
6. Name the device used in the first-violin melody in bars 59–62.
7. Suggest a reason why the timpani are not used in bars 66–69.
8. Explain how the role of the oboes in the texture of bars 66–69 differs from their various roles in the three sections of the Overture.
9. Outline the structure of the movement and explain where this passage occurs in it.

Now listen to two different recordings of this passage and comment on any similarities and differences that you notice. These might include pitch, tempo, dynamics, articulation, ornamentation, the type of ensemble and instruments used, and the balance between them.

Reception and interpretation

Bach enjoyed little fame as a composer in his lifetime. Very few of his works were published and many are thought to have been lost after his death in 1750. In his own day, he was better known for his skill as an organist.

An appreciation of Bach's music slowly began to develop in the second half of the 18th century, at first limited to small groups of professionals and connoisseurs. Beethoven, for example, played Bach's 48 Preludes and Fugues for keyboard, which he had learned from a manuscript copy and, following their first publication in 1801, recommended that they should be an essential part of a pianist's training. Interest in Bach's choral music was triggered in 1829 when the composer Mendelssohn conducted the first performance in over 100 years of Bach's largest-scale work, the *St Matthew Passion*. But it was not until the advent of recording in the early 20th century that much of Bach's output, especially his orchestral music, became widely known.

The Air from this suite is possibly Bach's best-known piece. It first became popular in a version known as 'The Air on the G string' because it was transposed down to be played in a rich, Romantic style, with lots of vibrato, entirely on the violin's lowest string. Another version, by the French jazz pianist Jacques Loussier, was used as background music to a long-running series of advertisements for cigars: the mood was one of contentment and relaxation, a man sitting back in his chair enjoying a small cigar, for which the music provided a sense of untroubled, unhurried reflection.

Even before you began to study this suite you may already have heard the Air performed in many different ways and settings. It has featured in numerous films and television programmes, and its association with weddings and funerals has given it an aura of almost quasi-religious devotion.

How does our response to performances that try to recreate the sort of sound that Bach would have heard compare to those that don't attempt to do this? It is scored for strings and continuo only, but how many players to a part do *you* think sounds best? Does it sound better played by solo instruments that allow the first violin to improvise additional ornaments freely? Do you prefer the sound of a large body of strings? Bach doesn't give crescendo or diminuendo markings in his music (and only rarely any basic indication of dynamic level) – does this mean it should be played at the same volume throughout? What about the repeats – louder or softer, or the same? How busy and prominent should the harpsichord be? Should string players use vibrato or not?

Further questions (in preparation for Section C)

1. What is the difference between natural trumpets and modern ones?
2. What features would you expect to hear in a historically-informed performance of Baroque music?
3. What are the characteristics of a French overture?

Mozart: Clarinet Concerto in A, K. 622

K. 622 is the number of this work in the catalogue of Mozart's works compiled by an Austrian scholar named Köchel.

This is one of the last works that Wolfgang Amadeus Mozart (1756–1791) completed. It was finished in October 1791, less than two months before the composer's death at the age of only 35. Mozart had visited Prague to oversee the performance of his new opera, *La clemenza di Tito*. His friend, the clarinettist Anton Stadler, stayed on in the city after Mozart had returned to Vienna, in order to give the first performance of this concerto on 16 October.

If you don't already have a score and CD of this work, the Eulenburg Audio + Score edition (EAS 36) offers a clear, modern score, packaged with a recording, at a competitive price.

The solo instrument

The autograph score of the concerto is lost, but an earlier draft of some of the first movement exists pitched a tone lower in G major. This shows that Mozart originally intended the solo part to be played on a **basset horn**, a type of clarinet that is lower in range than the standard instrument. When Mozart completed the work for Stadler, he transposed it to A major, but some notes are still too low for the modern clarinet in A. This is because the first performance was given on an instrument called the basset clarinet, devised by Stadler himself, which extends a 3rd below the bottom note of modern clarinets. When the concerto was eventually published in 1801 the lowest notes were moved up to suit the standard clarinet in A, but scholars have more recently been able to reconstruct Mozart's original intentions, based on the basset-horn draft.

Thea King plays the concerto on a basset clarinet on Hyperion CDA66199. The clarinettist Alan Hacker discusses the basset clarinet in his introduction to the miniature score published by Eulenburg as their edition ETP 778.

The late 18th century was an age of experiment and rapid development in instrument technology. Composers and performers were interested in extending the range of instruments, and in improving their intonation and reliability. They sought increased power, greater agility, and a wider range of tone colour and expressiveness. The piano displaced the harpsichord as the main keyboard instrument and various approaches were tried to improve wind instruments by adding or increasing the number of keys.

Although the clarinet had been heard increasingly across Europe during the second half of the 18th century, it was Mozart who first fully realised its potential and he used it whenever players were available. He had known and admired Stadler's playing for several years and they had become good friends. Mozart even referred to his quintet for clarinet and strings, written for the clarinettist in 1789, as the 'Stadler quintet'.

Mozart had first been excited by the possibilities of the clarinet when he heard them used in the court orchestra at Mannheim in Germany on a visit in 1788. He wrote enthusiastically to his father about the effect of hearing flutes, oboes *and* clarinets in a symphony.

The concerto

A concerto is a composition for orchestra in which one or more soloists have prominent parts. The solo music stands out from the orchestra's accompanying role by being technically more showy and often very expressive. Throughout the 1780s, when Mozart had been struggling financially and working hard to establish his reputation as a composer in Vienna, an important strand in his self-promotion was a steady stream of piano concertos, often for himself to play at his annual series of subscription concerts. He also composed concertos for many other solo instruments including piano, violin, flute, oboe, bassoon and horn.

In the late 18th century concertos consisted of three movements, in the order fast–slow–fast. The last of these was often an energetic, light-hearted **rondo**. The lively $^{6}_{8}$ of the last movement of the Clarinet Concerto is typical of Mozart's rondo finales.

Rondo

The basic principle of a rondo is that a main section, called the **refrain**, keeps coming back between slightly contrasting sections, called **episodes**. In this movement the soloist introduces the main themes while the orchestra supplies a discreet accompaniment and marks out the structure by rounding off sections with music of its own, sometimes joined by the soloist. Here is an outline:

Section	Bars	Principal keys
A	0^6–56	Tonic (A major)
B	57–114	Tonic → Dominant (E major *and* E minor)
(A)	114–137^5	Tonic → V of F♯ minor (the relative minor)
C $\frac{1}{2}$	137^6–178^1	F♯ minor → D major (subdominant)
(A)	177^6–187	D major → V of A major
B	188–246	Tonic (A major *and* A minor) → Dominant
A	247–301	Tonic (A major)
Coda	301–353	Tonic (A major). Bars 320^6–353 = A

If you use labels such as A and B in an exam answer you must first explain which themes or sections in the piece the letters refer to.

Sections shown as '(A)' are shortened versions of the refrain. The one starting in bar 177^6 is very short – just a snippet. Notice that the **coda** (a concluding section that affirms the tonic key) includes a final statement of the refrain.

The orchestra

The orchestra for Bach's Orchestral Suite No. 3 was big by Baroque standards, but by the end of the 18th century larger orchestras were becoming the norm, often including double woodwind, two horns, two trumpets and timpani, in addition to strings.

These larger resources were accompanied by changes in the style of orchestration. Whereas in Baroque music the bass line had an active, frequently contrapuntal role in the texture, in much Classical music the lower strings tend to provide supporting harmonies in a predominantly homophonic style. Woodwind are given short solo passages in addition to doubling violin melodies or providing harmonic support. In louder sections, the brass would thicken the middle of the harmony and sometimes provide some rhythmic punctuation as well. Horns and trumpets were still natural (valveless) instruments at this time.

All of these additional resources, many of which were used to bolster the harmonic foundation of the music, rendered a basso continuo part unnecessary, and the harpsichord dropped out of use in the Classical period.

Just as Bach's orchestra for the Orchestral Suite No. 3 was large for its day, so Mozart's for the Clarinet Concerto is quite small – no oboes, clarinets (other than the soloist), trumpets or drums – and its sound is more like that of a chamber music ensemble than a modern symphony orchestra. There is also little independent material for the woodwind in this movement – did Mozart do this to focus attention on the clarinet soloist? However, they all contribute to the general volume and energy of sound in the tutti passages and sometimes a flute or bassoon doubles a string part during a more lightly-scored passage. For example, in bars 73–76 unison bassoons double the chromatic line in the viola part; immediately after this, the first violin melody is doubled at the octave above by the first flute.

The two horns are not able to join in chromatic moments like these and are chiefly heard filling out tutti passages, often punctuating rhythmically on tonic or dominant notes. One delicate detail of Mozart's scoring for them occurs when they quietly double violins in bars 46–47 (and, again, in bars 292–293). This passage (shown *right* at sounding pitch) is such a typical way of writing for two natural horns that it is known as 'horn 5ths' or a 'horn call'.

The score

The solo clarinet and horn parts are pitched in A, and therefore sound a minor 3rd lower than written (compare the violin parts in bars 46–47 with the concert-pitch horn parts printed *above right*). Cellos and double-basses share a stave and play the same part (with the basses sounding an octave lower than written) except in a few short passages, such as bars 23–24 where Mozart wants a lighter texture.

Some of the exercises in earlier sections of this book have been taken from this score. It would be a good idea to look back at these to remind yourself of what they focused upon before continuing.

Exercise 22

Bars 1–4 are shown *below* in a reduced score with the solo clarinet at sounding pitch. Complete bars 5–8 in the same way, then listen to your recording to check that the sounds you have written match what you hear. (You will need three leger lines for the viola's low E in bar 7). Finally, identify each of the chords on the beats marked by a box.

Immediately after this opening statement of the main theme, the orchestra answers the soloist with its own version (bars 8^6–16). Notice how the woodwind and horns are used to increase the crescendo in bars 9–10 and 13–14. You will frequently hear this rhythmic motif punctuating the texture later in the movement – for example, bar 97 (horns, second violins and violas).

Exercise 23

Using your score, compare the orchestra's version of bars 8–16 with the soloist's opening in bars 1–8 and write down details of any aspect (rhythm, melody, harmony) that is different.

If you are intending to answer the questions on extract 1A in the exam, details of how music can be varied in quite a short space of time like this are worth looking out for.

Some of the differences are quite subtle:

- **Rhythm**: the semiquaver turn-like figure played by the soloist in bar 1 is reduced to repeated quavers in bar 9, and the motif in bar 3 is fragmented when it appears in bar 11. An adaptation of this new version then replaces the clarinet scales in bar 15.
- **Melody**: the first-violin melody in bar 10 goes up instead of down, and *vice versa* in bar 14. The flutes preserve the original direction both times but, when played by a modern orchestra with a large body of strings, this may not be clearly audible. Bar 4 has lost its chromaticism in the adaptation for bar 12.
- **Harmony**: the perfect cadence (V^7–I) of bar 2 is changed to an interrupted cadence (V^7–VI) in bar 10.

Practise reading the score *vertically* to get used to working out harmonies – check that you know exactly which instrument is playing each note of chord VI (F♯ minor) in bar 10. When does this chord next occur?

Tonality

You need to be confident about recognising the tonic key of A major and its most closely-related keys, E (the dominant), D (the sub-dominant) and F♯ minor (the relative minor).

The **harmonic rhythm** is often quite slow – one chord may last for quite a long time – particularly when the orchestra is quietly supporting the soloist in a display of scales or arpeggios (often referred to as 'passagework'). You may find that you can often feel the approach of a perfect cadence: practise spotting V^7–I and then common progressions such as Ic–V^7–I and IIb–V^7–I. Also practise identifying the keys (something you will need to be able to do accurately in Section B of the paper).

Although there are many passages of straightforward harmony, there are some where the music modulates rather freely, or even moves quickly through part of the circle of 5ths (see page 135). Mozart is very fond of chromaticism, both as a way of embellishing his melodies, as in the clarinet part of bars 149^6–153, and for enriching his harmonies, as in bars 179–183. You will not be expected to explain complex chords (such as those that use an augmented 6th) but it would be wise to learn to recognise when chromatic notes are present in a chord.

Commentary

A Bars 0^6–56

The opening statement of the principal theme is very compact, in fact quite similar to the sort of Classical theme that you might be asked about if you intend to choose extract 1A in the paper. You have already explored the scoring of its first 16 bars quite closely and its phrase structure was introduced on page 44.

At bar 16^6 there is a contrast. The strings play a simple harmonic framework that modulates sequentially to the dominant (V^7–I in A major in bars 17–18, then V^7–I in E major in bars 19–20). Above this the soloist begins the first technically showy passage of scales and broken chords.

Symmetrical phrasing is abandoned in this section: Mozart twice repeats the perfect cadence in the new key but immediately (bar 23) begins to head back towards the tonic – the D(♮) in the viola and cello parts is the clue – arriving on chord I in bar 24 after seven bars, rather than the expected eight. It is as though the brakes have gone on, calling the soloist to order after the stream of semiquavers, and is an example of the way in which Mozart could play on his listener's expectations, teasing the ear at the same time as driving the music onward into its next section.

Bars 23^6–31^1 restate the first eight bars, with some tiny alterations – try to identify these for yourself. Before the soloist can complete the last two notes of the theme, the orchestra enters on the first beat of bar 31 (again defying the listener's expectations), beginning a 'rounding-off' with five bars of perfect cadences in the tonic. In a carefully-crafted crescendo (the second violins and horns don't join in until bar 33) the violins pick up on the soloist's semiquavers. But Mozart is not quite ready to end the section: the soloist tries four bars of expressive melody which the orchestra interrupts forcefully in bar 40. The soloist tries again and manages eight bars before the orchestra completes the refrain.

B Bars 57–113

Although the clarinet melody beginning in bar 57 sounds like a new theme, there is no contrast in key (the music is still in the tonic key of A major at the start of this section) and Mozart has already hinted at the opening idea (compare the first-violin part in bar 57 with that in bar 46). Even the repeated quaver rhythm we first noticed in bar 9 resurfaces in the second violins at bar 58.

Mozart again starts with four balanced four-bar phrases (bars 57–72) but the modulation to the dominant key of E major that begins in bars 69–70 is followed by an abrupt modulation to the minor mode (E *minor*, bar 73). Notice the viola's chromatic descent in bars 73–76, which is taken up by the cellos and basses at bar 77.

Exercise 24

Compare the music of bars 77–81, and the way it is scored, with bars 73–76.

In a Classical concerto the soloist often signals the end of a flamboyant passage with a trill over the dominant chord, leading to a perfect cadence.

After some rich harmonies in bars 81–82 the clarinet gets into its semiquaver stride again, almost picking up from where the display of virtuosity left off in bar 72. The arpeggios become more energetic, commanding attention, and the outburst is rounded off with chromaticism and a cadential trill (bars 96–97).

The different registers of the clarinet were described on page 41.

The orchestra begins to close the section over a dominant pedal (notice the repeated E, in the familiar quaver rhythm, shared between lower strings and horns through bars 98–103), but the soloist wants the last word – three echoes of the chromatic scale from bar 95, each an octave lower than the last, descending deep into the **chalumeau** register (bars 105–109) before three huge leaps lead to a sustained dominant in bars 112–113.

(A) Bars 114–137[5]

The clarinet's dominant note, and a short chromatic ascent in the lower strings, lead to a very brief reminiscence of the refrain (A). After eight bars Mozart jumps straight to a tutti at bar 121 that repeats and extends the passage previously heard in bar 51. Strings maintain busy semiquaver movement throughout (often notated as a tremolando), entering in imitation in bars 125–130. From bar 127 onwards Mozart starts driving the music towards the relative minor (F♯ minor) in preparation for the next episode.

In bars 131–132 the basic rhythm of $\frac{6}{8}$ (two groups of three quavers) is changed to three groups of two quavers – a technique known as **hemiola** (see *left*). The dominant of F♯ minor is then repeated as a pedal throughout bars 134–137, ending with bare octaves on C♯, preparing for the key of the next section.

C Bars 137[6]–178[1]

At the start of this action-packed episode the soloist introduces a new, contrasting theme (C[1]) in the relative minor (bars 137[6]–158). Its first eight bars are repeated an octave lower, starting at bar 145[6], reaching an imperfect cadence in bar 153 (chord V of F♯ minor). The bass figure introduced in this bar then alternates in **dialogue** with the clarinet. Is there once again a reference to earlier material? Compare this fragment with the second-violin part in bars 73–77 (and the following four bars for clarinet).

The familiar repeated quavers punctuate and define the end of a passage (bar 157) but, this time, Mozart dramatically repeats them in a new guise in the next bar, turning the tonality in a totally unexpected direction: the C♯ that in bar 157 was the dominant of F♯ minor becomes the leading note of D major in bar 158. The imminent arrival of a new key is confirmed by the chord above the C♯ in the bass, which is V^7 of D major, the subdominant key.

The soloist, too, enters in a dramatic way, with a wide leap of nearly two octaves and a helter-skelter down a scale of D major before developing these wide leaps into an apparently new theme (C[2]). But this loses momentum after eight bars (bars 161–168) as it moves sequentially through a **diatonic circle of 5ths** (see page 135): follow the bass line from bar 168: A–D–G♮–C♯–F♯–B–E–A. The episode comes to an end with a perfect cadence in D major (Ic–V–I) and another cadential trill from the clarinet (bar 177–178).

(A) Bars 177[6]–187

The soloist's trill overlaps with the start of a brief reference to A, beginning at bar 177[6]. These eight bars are complex: imitative, sequential, richly-harmonised, chromatic and modulating – review Exercise 13 on page 55 and the suggested answers on page 58. At the end of this tightly-compressed passage Mozart arrives on a dominant chord of E major (bars 186–187) in preparation for the return of the tonic key and full restatements of the opening two sections of the movement in reverse order.

Because this return of section A is very short and not in the tonic key, you may see commentaries that regard these bars as being part of episode C.

B Bars 188–246

Bars 188–195 are the same as bars 57–64, suggesting that Mozart is about to repeat his first episode B, but at bar 196 he plunges without warning into the tonic minor (A minor) in a gesture that parallels the change of mode from E major to E minor in the earlier episode (bar 73), but now a 5th lower and much earlier than expected.

The music then modulates rapidly from A minor, through C major (bar 200) to chord V of D minor in bar 207. A pair of octave leaps in that bar return the clarinet to its high register for a sequential passage (bars 208–213) that returns to A minor.

Exercise 25

1. In as much detail as you can, describe the texture of the music in bars 196–207. Refer precisely to instruments and bar numbers in your answer.
2. Compare the music of bars 214–230 with that of bars 73–97. Explain the similarities and differences as fully as you can.

After completing this exercise, you should have a clear idea of how Mozart reuses and varies earlier music in this episode. However, notice that he doesn't repeat the most virtuoso passage from the earlier B episode (bars 88–96), because he wants to reserve his most brilliant fireworks for the coda. At bar 230 Mozart begins an exact repetition of bar 97–113, now in its original key.

A Bars 247–301

Bars 247–301 are an almost exact reprise of the first refrain (without the opening anacrusis).

Coda (including A) Bars 301–353

The coda begins with a spectacular display of virtuosity by the soloist (bars 301–322). Material from section A returns at bar 322, in a sequential dialogue between strings and clarinet derived from bar 178 in the second episode. Even at this late stage in the movement Mozart still has an appetite for varying this theme. At last he settles into the home straight, with a final appearance of the principal eight-bar theme of the refrain, starting in bar 334. Its final note is changed to rise to the dominant in bar 341, launching a brief extension that includes more huge leaps and a cadential trill for the clarinet (bars 344–345). The final bars are based on the tutti from bar 121, the repeated V^7–I progressions reinforcing the home key of A major.

Interpretation

On most recordings the solo instrument is a clarinet in A. Now that scores are available which include what was probably the original notation for Stadler's basset clarinet, clarinettists have shown an interest in performing the concerto on either that instrument or on a basset horn. You should therefore be prepared for the possibility that some of the solo passages on a recording might differ from the score that you use. The reconstructed original extends the range of the instrument down by a 3rd (to written C, sounding A), allowing its expressive lowest notes to be appreciated and making better musical sense in arpeggio passages such as this:

Practice test

Listen to the passage in bars 121–137 while following the score, and then answer the following questions:

1. What is the sounding pitch of the octave played by the horns in bar 128?
2. Explain the marking *zu 2* (or *a 2*) in the flute parts at bar 129.
3. Describe the texture of bars 125–129.
4. Write out the viola part in bars 131–132 as it would actually be performed and using a treble clef.
5. What rhythmic device is used in bars 131–132?
6. Name the key in which the passage begins at bar 121 and the key of bars 129–130.
7. Identify the chord in bar 136.
8. Comment on the texture of bar 137.
9. Explain where in the structure of the whole movement this passage comes from and describe briefly what comes next. Try to do this without consulting the score.

Now listen to two different recordings of this passage and comment on any similarities and differences that you notice. These might include tempo, dynamics, articulation, ornamentation, the type of ensemble and instruments used, and the balance between them.

Further questions (in preparation for Section C)

1. What sort of instrument was this concerto originally intended for?
2. Which woodwind and brass instruments are used in the orchestra?
3. Discuss, with examples, the virtuosity of the solo part.

Schubert: Symphony No. 8 in B minor, D. 759

This symphony is commonly known as 'Schubert's *Unfinished*', a nickname arising from the fact that the composer never completed the last two of the work's four movements, although he did leave sketches for the third movement. You may see it described as 'op. posth.' which means that the work ('opus') was not published until after the composer's death ('posthumous'). You might also see the work described as Schubert's Symphony No. 7, since this was the number assigned to it when Schubert's symphonies were renumbered in 1978.

D. 759 is the work's number in the standard catalogue of Schubert's music, compiled by Otto Deutsch.

If you don't already have a score and CD of this work, the Eulenburg Audio + Score edition (EAS 129) offers a clear, modern score, packaged with a recording, at a competitive price. This score, like the *Urtext* edition from Bärenreiter (TP 407), entitles the work 'Symphony No. 7'.

A great many symphonies were written in the last 30 years of the 18th century, and their popularity continued throughout the 19th and into the 20th centuries. They are substantial compositions for orchestra, usually in four movements. The first movement was fairly fast and often the weightiest, the second slow, the third a minuet (or, later, a scherzo) and trio, and the last was usually fast and lively to round the whole thing off.

Scholars and biographers have always been puzzled over why Franz Schubert (1797–1828) never finished this symphony, given the quality of its two completed movements. It is known that Schubert became quite ill after composing these in October 1822 and this may have been the reason. In 1823 he gave the score of the two movements to a friend as a thank-you present but, as far as we know, he never heard the work performed, not even in rehearsal.

Schubert did, in fact, leave a number of works unfinished, including many of his piano sonatas, and there were several other abandoned attempts at writing symphonies.

Sonata form

In the second half of the 18th century a musical form evolved that was widely adopted for the first movement of symphonies, trios, quartets and sonatas for solo instruments. When theorists studied it in later centuries it became known as **Sonata form** or 'first-movement form'. In fact, its use wasn't confined to first movements – it was often adapted for slow movements and finales, and used for single-movement works such as overtures.

Sonata form grew out of binary form, which had already started to become longer due to an increasing tendency to round off the ending by repeating material from the first section, modified to end in the tonic.

As the Baroque principle of a single *affekt* (or mood) for a piece gradually gave way to Classical styles, composers began including a second theme, designed to give greater importance to the related key in which the first section ends and which was often designed to *contrast* with the first theme.

The result became the first section (known as the **exposition**) of sonata form: a **first subject** in the tonic key followed by a **second subject** in a related key (which was normally the dominant in a major-key movement or the relative major in a minor key). The whole of this exposition is repeated, just as the first section of a binary-form movement is repeated.

After the repeat sign the composer was free to develop (vary) the themes and other figures from the exposition in a section called the **development**. In this, composers would modulate fairly freely and manipulate their thematic material in various ways, often exploring small motifs taken from themes in the exposition. Towards the end of the development, a passage of **dominant preparation**, often involving a **dominant pedal**, would prepare the way for the return of the tonic key.

The final section is the **recapitulation**, in which the themes from the exposition are restated in their original order but with one essential difference: to ensure that the movement ends in the home key, the second subject is changed to appear in the tonic. At the end there is usually a **coda** (literally, a 'tail'), designed to reaffirm the tonic key after the tonal explorations of the development.

Tonality

B minor, the tonic key of the work, had rarely been used for orchestral music. It has been noted that Schubert's songs in this key often deal with subjects of alienation and despair. At the time that Schubert was composing there was much interest in a theory of how each key might suggest a specific colour. Beethoven is said to have described the colour of B minor as 'black'.

A characteristic trait of Schubert's style is switching between major and minor modes of the same tonic key.

The structure of Schubert's first movement is straightforward: sonata form with a significant coda. But the music is very eventful and a notable feature is its unusual key relationships:

- In the exposition the first subject (a group of two themes) is in the tonic key of B minor, but the second subject is in the somewhat distant key of G major, to which Schubert abruptly modulates.
- In the recapitulation the introductory theme of the first subject is omitted and the first subject ends in the dominant (F♯ minor). The second subject then follows in D major (the relative major of the home key) rather than the more usual tonic, although the final references to the second subject are in the tonic major (B major).
- The coda is introduced by music from the end of the exposition and it brings back the introductory theme that had been omitted from the recapitulation. This creates a moment's doubt that the movement may be about to repeat from the beginning of the development instead of coming to a close. However, there is no repeat of the second part of this movement.

A summary of the sonata-form structure of the movement is shown in the table *opposite*.

Orchestra

The inclusion of three trombones in the orchestra is an indication that Schubert was thinking on a grand scale. They had been used in church music and opera in the 18th century, but were not introduced into symphonies until the 19th century (most notably by Beethoven in 1808). Unlike the trumpets and horns of the day, they could play chromatically and were, therefore, more versatile melodically. In bars 176–197 they dramatically double the cellos and basses. Even so, their principal role was to give dark colouring to noisy passages. They are used as a 'choir' (supplying three-part harmonies) and often provide stabbing accents, as in bars 162–165.

Exposition			
Bars 1–8 Bars 9–38	B minor (tonic)	**A1** **A2**	First subject: Introductory theme Principal theme
Bars 38–42	Modulating link		
Bars 42–93 Bars 93–104	G major (submediant)	**B**	Second subject Closing section
Bars 104–110	Modulating link		
Development			
Bars 111–114	Modulating link		
Bars 114–218	E minor + modulations		A1 (mostly)
Recapitulation			
Bars 218–252	B minor	**A2**	First subject (principal theme) extended to end on V
Bars 252–256	Modulating link		Similar to bars 38–42 in the exposition
Bars 256–311 Bars 311–322	D major (relative major) B major (tonic major)	**B**	Second subject Closing section
Bars 322–328	B minor (link to coda)		Similar to bars 104–110 in the exposition
Coda			
Bars 328–368	B minor	**A1**	

Apart from the trombones Schubert's orchestra is not unusual for its date: double woodwind (two each of flutes, oboes, clarinets and bassoons), two horns, two trumpets, timpani and strings.

There are several passages where double-basses are independent of the cellos, such as in bars 42–61, where their pizzicato notes provide the roots of the harmony while cellos play the legato theme above them. Remember that double basses sound an octave lower than notated. Passages that descend below the bottom E of the standard double bass (such as bars 122–131) require either a five-string double bass, or a bass with a 'C extension'.

Individual woodwind instruments have very few solo moments and Schubert makes little use of their expressive potential: in bars 13–20 the first oboe and first clarinet introduce the principal theme in unison, but are otherwise mainly used to reinforce the harmonies in support of the strings. Clarinets (doubled an octave lower by violas) provide an important syncopated accompaniment to the second subject, starting in bar 42. At bar 53 bassoons replace the violas – notice how the horns add further rhythmic interest to the syncopation with their pedal note on D.

> Notice that the clarinets are in A, so they sound a minor 3rd lower than written, like the solo part in Mozart's Clarinet Concerto.

Trumpets and horns with piston valves had started to appear just before this symphony was written, but were not widely available and most composers (including Schubert) continued to write for natural brass for some years to come. However, natural brass poses problems in minor keys, since the available pitches are those of a major scale (see the examples in the margin of page 64). To help get round this difficulty, Schubert directs the horns to crook in D, sounding a minor 7th lower than written. The trumpets are crooked in E, sounding a major 3rd higher than notated, but they play very little in this movement. The two timpani are tuned to the tonic and dominant of B minor (B and F♯).

Schubert's themes, and the way he scores them, tend to be more intentionally expressive (and therefore more Romantic) than those of his immediate predecessors. In comparison with the music of Bach or Mozart, his orchestral sounds may seem more colourful, with strong contrasts between dark and sunny effects. Some of Schubert's scoring decisions reflect the influence of the tonal scheme – for example, the trumpets in E are used mainly to articulate the rhythm and bolster the weight of orchestral sound in the development, part of which is in E minor. The following commentary highlights some of the details of the scoring.

Commentary

Exposition

Music in Baroque and Classical styles usually kicks off confidently with a strong theme that establishes the tonic key straight away, but Schubert begins this movement extremely quietly with an introductory theme (**A1**) that we have to strain our ears to hear, very low down in the cellos and basses. The lack of harmony around it means that we are not sure about B minor until the upper strings join them in bar 9. This theme returns in bar 328, near the end of the movement, and this final appearance starts in exactly the same way – cellos and basses in octaves, alone, low, soft and smooth.

Let's compare the two passages. The opening phrase ends on a sustained dominant (F♯ in bars 6–8), which seems to be waiting for something to happen. In the corresponding place in the coda (bars 333–335) the F♯ supports a Ic–V^7–I cadence added above it by hushed woodwind and brass. This is the clue that the movement is ending, not starting from the beginning all over again.

Schubert, who is perhaps best known as a song writer, often let the piano set the scene before the voice enters in his songs. The same technique is used again in bars 42–43 to introduce the second subject.

Returning to the exposition, in bar 9 rustling strings get things moving with a new figure (the principal theme, **A2**). They gradually emerge after the mysterious opening, as though they were playing the introduction in an accompaniment to a song. The 'singer' – oboe and clarinet in unison – enters with the melody at bar 13. Notice how, without interrupting the flow of the music, the ***fz*** interjection of the horns and trombone in bar 20 gradually gets taken up by the woodwind who seem to urge the strings on, in a long crescendo that culminates in a ***ff*** perfect cadence in the tonic key at bar 38.

Exercise 26

1. Look at the score to see where Schubert marks the lower strings (including viola) pizzicato and arco in bars 9–38, then listen hard to the passage, trying to hear the difference and how it contributes to the crescendo effect.
2. This passage returns in the recapitulation but Schubert extends it to engineer the change of key. Compare the music and scoring of bars 218–252 with bars 9–38, noting the similarities and differences.

Having ended his first group of themes in the tonic, Schubert has to find a way of moving to a different key for the second subject. Bars 38–42 bring about an almost instant modulation from B minor to G major by using the sustained D in bassoons and horns as a pivot note – it starts out as the 3rd of the tonic chord of B minor, is held in a sort of unharmonised no-man's land and is then quitted as though it were the dominant of the new key, G major.

Exercise 27

Write out bars 38^2–42^1 on a single stave in the treble clef, at sounding pitch. Remember that the horns are pitched in D, and notice that bassoons have moved into the tenor clef.

The effect of this short link is not only to change the key but also to change the mood. Following the loud, strongly rhythmic tutti, the texture collapses onto a single note and the dynamic fades to ***pp*** in the space of only four bars. Although the keys involved at the equivalent spot in the recapitulation are different, exactly the same process is used in bars 252^2–256^1 to take the music to D major.

To introduce the second subject, Schubert again sets an accompaniment figure in motion first (bars 42–43): pizzicato double basses mark the first beat of each bar with either I or V of the new key (G major), while violas, doubled an octave above by clarinets, suggest the harmonies in a gently syncopated rhythm. This rhythm recurs several times elsewhere in the movement.

The theme is announced by the cellos, starting in bar 44. When it passes to the violins in octaves, the cellos recede into the harmonic background, but notice how Schubert accents the second beats of bars 53 and 54, in rhythmic counterpoint to the melody. The horns add a further rhythmic dimension, with syncopations that interlock with the woodwind – note the detail of how they sustain *across* the bar lines, making the accompaniment more continuous.

Schubert interrupts the smooth flow of the second subject with an unexpected silence in bar 62 where our ears expect a quiet chord of G major. This is immediately followed by a dramatic, very loud and heavily-accented passage, with strings playing tremolo.

A total silence, as in bar 62, is often called a **general pause**, although there is no actual pause in the pulse.

Exercise 28

1. Identify the chord played in bar 63.
2. Suggest a reason why the trumpets and timpani do not contribute to the powerful orchestral entry in bar 63.

Woodwind syncopations resume with a rapid diminuendo and in bar 73 strings pick-up the conversation with the *third* bar of the melody (almost in a spirit of '... as I was saying, before I was so rudely interrupted ...'). This bar is treated in imitative sequence between different combinations of string instruments, some at the unison (violas and cellos) others at the octave (first and second violins). Notice the abrupt change in dynamic and articulation when the basses enter.

It is unusual for such dramatic contrasts and shifting modulations to occur in an exposition. It is almost as though Schubert has begun to develop the second subject before he gets to the development – but then, apart from using its syncopated accompaniment figure, he leaves it out of the actual development section.

Bars 93–104 could be described as a codetta (a short coda).

Notice that more dramatic chords appear briefly to make a strongly-articulated cadence in G major at bars 92–93. After this, strings and woodwind share a last, delicately scored and nostalgic look at the second subject in a brief closing section. In the recapitulation, the scoring of this passage (bars 311–322) is subtly different.

Exercise 29

1. Identify the five chords played in bars 87^2–89^1. Which harmonies are different when the cadence is repeated in bars 91^2–93^1?
2. Compare the scoring of the closing sections of the exposition (bars 93–104) and the recapitulation (bars 311–322).

Development

The development section of a sonata-form movement was one where a composer might choose to explore the potential of *any* theme from the exposition. It would not be varied in the sense of a formal set of variations – more commonly small fragments from themes would be manipulated in various ways – presented in new keys, alternative textures or different orchestration. Schubert bases almost the entire development section on his introductory theme (**A1**) and builds it up in a long crescendo to a powerful climax:

Quotations from *Schubert and the Symphony: A New Perspective* by Brian Newbould. Toccata Press, 1990, ISBN 0-907689-27-2, pages 194–195.

- Bar 114. Cellos and basses as at the beginning of the movement, but in E minor and without the final sustained note. Instead they carry on down the scale to a very low C♮, a note which seems to open the door to a new sound world. The Schubert scholar Brian Newbould has drawn attention to the way 'the *tremolando* intensifies the mystery of this new remote region' and the 'vast textural hollow' created by the gap between top and bottom notes when the violins enter in bar 122.
- Bar 122. Violins in octaves begin **A1** but they get hooked on a falling semitone figure (B–A♯) which they develop right through to bar 146.
- Bar 124. Violas doubled by bassoons imitate the violins.
- Bar 134. More wind join in; double basses separate from cellos; notice the trombone accentuation and rhythm, and the way the music builds up from bar 114 to bar 146.
- Bars 146–170. Chords melt into the accompaniment rhythm of **B** (but without the actual second-subject melody). This dramatic gesture is repeated sequentially twice more.

- Bar 170. **A1** returns, tutti and ***ff***. The key is once again E minor.
- Bar 176. Trombones in octaves join the cellos and basses on **A1**, imitated by woodwind, while upper strings rush about in semiquavers introducing a new mood of urgent activity.
- Bar 184. A powerful tutti in which driving, dotted rhythms and imitative figures are combined with bars 3–5 of **A1** played by cellos, basses and trombones. This combination is repeated in a free modulating sequence, leading to …
- Bar 194. A climax of activity. The two-bar figure is marked ***ffz***, then ***fz***, finally ***pp***, and the scoring reduces.
- Bar 208. A slow relaxation, preparing for the return of **A2**, over dominant pedal in the horns.

Recapitulation

Since **A1** has been so prominent in the development, and Schubert intends to come back to it in the coda, he leaves it out at the beginning of the recapitulation. But **A2** and the transition to **B** follow along similar lines to the exposition. **B** itself is in the unexpected key of D major (a 5th higher than its first appearance, and the relative major of the main key). Schubert extends the end of this melody with a sequence that sounds as though he is on his way back to the tonic key, B minor (bars 276–279). The principal difference in scoring is that flutes join clarinets in the syncopated figure (bar 256) and violas drop out – the effect is a little brighter. But, although the material is the same as before, the final passage (beginning at bar 291) is in the much brighter key of B *major*.

Coda

The music of the coda (staring in bar 328) recalls the opening of the development section. To lead into it, Schubert makes exactly the same link as he had made between the end of the exposition and the beginning of the development (bar 106 – sustained wind, tonic pedal, pizzicato strings descending in unison).

Exercise 30

Compare Schubert's use of the introductory theme (**A1**) in the coda with how it appears at the beginning of the development section. Comment on his scoring, use of dynamics, articulation and performing techniques.

Reception and interpretation

Why did Schubert start work on this symphony? By 1822 his reputation as a composer was spreading fast in cultured Viennese circles. The previous year one of his most famous and innovative songs, *Der Erlkönig*, had caused a considerable stir.

Of the four composers sometimes referred to as the 'First Viennese School' (Haydn, Mozart and Beethoven being the others), Schubert is the only one who was actually born in the city. He grew up surrounded by music. It was common for sometimes quite large instrumental ensembles, made up of family and friends, to gather to perform at home. Schubert had been composing prolifically from his mid teens onwards – choral, chamber, piano and orchestral music – but it was as an outstanding composer of *Lieder* (German songs) that his abilities particularly marked him out.

However, while Schubert had composed a number of small-scale symphonies, by 1822 he was beginning to have more ambitious aspirations. He wanted to be known as a serious composer, and was beginning to realise that in order to make people really sit up and take notice, he needed to write a 'grand' symphony. In fact, Schubert did subsequently finish such a work, although it was not performed during his lifetime: Symphony No. 9, now known as the 'Great C major'.

In 1824 Schubert wrote to a friend that he was intending to write a large-scale symphony so that he could put on a big concert similar to those mounted by Beethoven: 'I intend to pave my way towards a grand symphony ... The latest in Vienna is that Beethoven is to give a concert at which he is to produce his new symphony ... I too am thinking of giving a similar concert next year.'

Schubert was 31 years old when he died. Like Mozart, his death came at a moment when his music was beginning to attract wider public acclaim and success seemed to be within his grasp. Only the year before he had carried a torch at Beethoven's funeral, when thousands of people had lined the streets. Because Schubert had never sought to make a reputation for himself as a performer, and his grand concert never did materialise, it was initially a much narrower circle that mourned him. His music had chiefly been performed by a growing band of enthusiastic friends in private houses.

After Schubert's death the reputation of his songs spread rapidly and they proved to be very influential in raising the status of German *Lieder* to that of major art-works. Several of his shorter piano pieces remained popular, but most of the orchestral works disappeared from view until the composer Mendelssohn gave the first performance of the 'Great C-major' Symphony in 1839.

Much of the credit for recognising the stature of Schubert's music goes to another German composer, Robert Schumann, and to a Hungarian one, Franz Liszt, both generous in their promotion of other composers. Austrians increasingly realised what might have been, had Schubert lived longer. As some of his music became better known he was belatedly seen as the lost heir to Beethoven.

It was in this atmosphere that the manuscript of the *Unfinished* Symphony was brought out and the first performance given to great acclaim on 17 December 1865 in Vienna. This first performance in his native country was followed two years later by its introduction to British audiences by George Grove at the Crystal Palace in London. Thereafter a sort of Schubert-mania took hold.

An account of the first performance is given on page 249 of the *Cambridge Companion to Schubert* edited by Christopher H. Gibbs. Cambridge University Press, 1997, ISBN 0-521-48424-3.

In the 20th century scholars took a more critical view of Schubert's handling of sonata form (in his sonatas and quartets as well as the symphonies). Just as Schubert might have feared, unfavourable comparisons began to be made with Beethoven's music. But his ready gift for an instantly singable, memorable tune made some of his music very accessible to a wider public.

Schubert's biography was viewed as a typical Romantic tragedy – the life of a talented artist cut short before he could realise his full potential, and was often treated very sentimentally in literature and on the screen. This sort of treatment has, in turn, tended to colour the interpretation and reception of Schubert's music. It is common for commentators to refer to 'dark forebodings', or 'death as a constant companion', or 'resigned acceptance of his fate' (and certainly many of the poems he chose to set to music in his songs do have a tragic tone). Perhaps this incomplete symphony remains popular today because of the direct way in which most listeners feel that Schubert speaks personally through his music. What does it say to you?

Practice test

Study bars 281–311 in the score and answer the following questions:

1. Explain the notation of the string parts in bar 281.
2. Identify the chord played in bar 283.
3. Write out in the treble clef the music played by violas and cellos in bars 291–292.
4. Describe the relationship between the flutes and clarinets between bars 291–298.
5. Comment on the texture and scoring of the passage in bars 291–303.
6. In what key does this passage end in bar 311?

Now put the score away and answer the following two questions from memory:

7. From which part of the movement does this passage come?
8. Briefly indicate what happens after the end of this passage.

Finally, listen to two different recordings of this passage and comment on any similarities and differences that you notice. These might include pitch, tempo, dynamics, articulation, ornamentation, the type of ensemble and instruments used, and the balance between them.

Further questions (in preparation for Section C)

1. In what ways were the orchestral textures available to Schubert different from those used by Bach and Mozart?
2. Discuss two short passages from this work that you consider to be examples of effective orchestration.

Jazz recordings

Instrumental jazz, 1920–1960

At the beginning of the 1920s jazz was beginning to establish itself as a distinctive style of music. Musicians from New Orleans, the birthplace of jazz, were being drawn to the big cities of America, especially New York and Chicago, and the new technologies of recording and radio broadcasting were beginning to spread the sound of jazz throughout the United States and all over the world.

This is not the same as saying that jazz itself was over by 1960! Jazz standards continue to be played and new jazz performers continue to develop their styles.

By 1960, the era in which jazz had often dominated popular music was over. There had been many rapid changes in the intervening 40 years – new musical styles had travelled far and caught on quickly. Compare this with the slower development of musical ideas in the 18th and 19th centuries, when Bach, Mozart and Schubert were composing.

Although jazz changed rapidly, you should not assume that later styles were better than earlier ones. Although we tend to talk of music 'developing', this means only that one style tended to grow out of another in sequence. There's no reason to suppose that Miles Davis is 'better' than Louis Armstrong or Jelly Roll Morton simply because he was working 30 years later. All of the jazz musicians you will be studying were among the best of their day, working with the styles and techniques of the time.

Listening to the jazz recordings

Try to get copies of the specified recordings for each of the three works you will be studying (see the list on page 59). Take your time to get to know each work well. Jazz can seem confusing when you first hear it, but repeated listening will help you to make sense of the music. Discussing what you hear with others and working through the sections in this book will also help you.

In the exam you will only have an extract from the recording to work from. There will be no score to follow. In this book the structure of each work is laid out in a table, with the timing in minutes and seconds. There are also some musical examples, which are transcribed from the recordings.

The transcriptions are only a guide. Jazz scores are not as reliable as classical scores as it is impossible to notate all of the nuances of pitch and rhythm heard in jazz. Many jazz composers use only outline instrumental parts and communicate many of their ideas verbally. Improvised sections in your set works were not written down. You will need to listen carefully to hear how the recorded performance differs from what is written. The tables and examples are there to help you to get to know the work better.

Once you know your way around the work, put the examples and timings aside. Getting to know the work by ear is vital.

Key features of jazz

Frontline. These are the instruments that play the melody line. New Orleans jazz of the 1920s used trumpet, clarinet and trombone. The saxophone overtook the clarinet in popularity in the 1930s.

Rhythm section. This usually consists of drums, piano, banjo (or guitar in later jazz) and bass. The bass was usually a double bass played pizzicato (plucked) although the more powerful sound of a tuba was often used on early recordings. Sometimes the left hand of the pianist provides the bass. Chords are played by the piano and banjo or guitar. Players would often fill out the harmonies by adding extra notes, fills and syncopated rhythms – a technique called **comping** (an abbreviation of 'accompanying').

Walking bass. A bass part, usually improvised, of four steady crotchets per bar, in which chord notes are often linked by passing notes to produce mainly stepwise movement. Earlier examples, from the late 1930s, are often quite simple but by the 1950s bass players were getting more adventurous in exploring the different registers of the instrument, giving their bass lines a character that matched the changing moods of the music as a whole.

The bass in the earliest jazz tended to be in two-beat rhythm, reflecting its ragtime and march origins. The four-beat pattern developed with the rise of the double bass as the main bass instrument.

Improvisation. The ability to make-up and vary passages while performing, rather than reading them note by note from a copy, is an essential skill for a jazz musician. Improvisation often involves some degree of preparation of basic ideas and, in jazz, is usually based on an underlying chord pattern.

Arrangement. Not all jazz is improvised. Most of the works you are studying have an element of pre-composition. A jazz musician would need to be able to read music to make a living playing in the clubs and theatres of New York or Chicago. Written arrangements helped to improve standards of ensemble in the bigger bands.

Swing. Jazz is well known for its exciting rhythms. Early jazz reflected the syncopations of ragtime. In the 1920s, jazz musicians started replacing pairs of even quavers (known as **straight eights**) with a more lilting style in which the first quaver of each pair is held longer than the second. In addition, notes would often be anticipated or delayed in relation to the strictly maintained beat of the rhythm section. Swing is difficult to define or notate, and not everyone will agree whether a performance is swung or not.

Changes. Many jazz pieces are based on a repeating chord pattern known as the changes. Each repetition of the chord progression is known as a **chorus**. One of the best-known changes is the chord pattern of the 12-bar blues. Others are often based on the harmonies of well-known popular songs of the time, known as **standards**, many of which are in 32-bar song form (AABA).

Basing variations on a repeating chord structure is a composing technique that has been used for centuries. In jazz, the practice of borrowing just the chords of a standard, without the tune, developed originally as a way to avoid infringing the copyright of the popular song being used.

Blue notes and inflections. Listen out for small alterations in the pitch of notes. The most common are blue notes, involving a slight flattening of the 3rd, 5th or 7th degree of the scale. A keyboard instrument gives a poor impression of how these should sound. Listen to a jazz wind player or singer and see if you can hear the pitch of certain notes being pushed higher or lower for expressive effect. The pitch can also be bent while a note is being played.

Tone quality. Jazz musicians use many ways to vary the sound of their instruments, including different types of attack, production (such as deliberately rough or breathy tone), and vibrato (early jazz players used a fast vibrato, but the later works you are studying have slower vibrato). Mutes are often used to change the sound of brass instruments. Originally a mute could be a piece of cloth, a hat or any item which came to hand. The most common mutes today are the straight, cup, Harmon and plunger.

Double time. Playing in semiquavers instead of the usual quavers.

Recording technology

Securing a recording contract became an increasingly important part of the business of making jazz. Record sales generated larger audiences to hear live performances, which in turn offered the chance to secure bigger contracts with other companies later.

By 1920 the gramophone record had become the main way of bringing music to a wider audience, although it was soon to be joined by the newly developing medium of radio broadcasting. Recording companies spurred on the development of jazz by competing to search out new music and find artists who would be commercially successful.

Recording for the gramophone was originally an acoustic process, involving the use of a large recording horn that would capture the vibrations of the sound and record them as patterns on a wax disc. This would then be used to produce a mould from which multiple copies could be stamped onto brittle discs made from a naturally occuring compound called shellac. A shellac record was limited to three minutes of music on each side, which forced musicians to organise their pieces more compactly than they would in a live situation.

These early acoustic recordings suffered from problems of musical balance. The soloist(s) had to be placed close to the recording horn to be heard, and drums and bass instruments were difficult to record adequately – hence the reason why a tuba often replaced the double bass in the early years of recording.

Following the development of the first microphones suitable for music, electrical recording rapidly replaced the older acoustic method after 1925. The earliest works you are studying benefitted from this new process, although the end product was still a shellac disc with limited play time. Microphones improved in quality, and were soon able to cope with the bigger bands of the 1930s.

The development of tape recording and the LP (long-playing) record in the late 1940s revolutionised the record industry. Each side of an LP record offered at least 20 minutes of uninterrupted playing time, allowing jazz musicians to develop their ideas over a much longer period. Tape recording was equally revolutionary, since it became possible to edit and splice together sections recorded at different times, rather than always having to capture a complete performance in a single take. Furthermore, sound engineers could exercise better control of recording conditions, placing individual microphones in different positions so that the performance could be artificially balanced. This allowed instrumental combinations which would not be practical in a live situation. The work of the sound engineer also became increasingly important with the advent of stereo recording in the 1950s, towards the end of our period.

Further reading on jazz

Jazz by Mervyn Cooke. Thames and Hudson, 1998, ISBN 978-0-500203-18-7. A short, attractively presented guide to the history of jazz.

Jazz Styles: History and Analysis by Mark C. Gridley. Prentice Hall, 1978/2008, ISBN 978-0-136005-89-6. A detailed introduction to jazz for American college students. CDs are available separately to accompany the latest edition.

What to listen for in Jazz by Barry Kernfeld. Yale University Press, 1995, ISBN 978-0-300059-02-1. Looks at musical elements of jazz, with a range of examples on an accompanying CD, including *Black Bottom Stomp, Jumpin' at the Woodside* and *Ko-Ko.*

A New History of Jazz by Alyn Shipton. Continuum, 1988/2007, ISBN 978-0-826417-89-3. An excellent and readable history.

Jelly Roll Morton: *Black Bottom Stomp*

This is one of the three jazz recordings set for exams in June 2009, January and June 2010, and January 2011.

If you are taking the exam in June 2011 or later, turn to the section starting on page 114.

Jelly Roll Morton (died 1941) was not only one of the most colourful of personalities in early jazz but also its first great composer. Born Ferdinand Lemott in New Orleans at an uncertain date between 1885 and 1890, he grew up in a Creole (mixed-race) family and as a young man spent much of his time in the red-light district of Storyville, particularly the white part where few black musicians would go.

There he worked as a pianist in the local brothels, and several of his ragtime piano pieces were published in the first decade of the 20th century, but he earned much of his living from procuring clients for prostitutes and relieving them of even more money by luring them into gambling. 'Jelly Roll' cultivated the image of a showman, changing outfits several times a day, presenting himself as a big spender who sported a diamond in one tooth and carried large amounts of cash. Morton's family disowned him and he left New Orleans when Storyville was closed down in 1917. After travelling widely, Morton settled in Chicago in 1923 where a huge public demand for jazz was growing rapidly.

Morton later exaggerated his role in the development of jazz, claiming to have invented it single-handedly in 1902. Nevertheless, his contribution as the first great jazz composer was considerable. He composed, published, cut piano rolls (one of the precursors of the gramophone record) and later made studio recordings of his works.

Jelly Roll Morton experimented with structure, breaking away from the predictability of ragtime and interspersing the passages of collective improvisation characteristic of New Orleans jazz with short solo sections. Morton's Chicago recordings established new standards of professionalism and ensemble in jazz. Pieces such as *King Porter Stomp* became standards which were later arranged by others. However, by the end of the 1920s, Morton's style of jazz was eclipsed in popularity by the easy melodic style of the big bands with their sophisticated harmonies and instrumentation.

The recording

Black Bottom Stomp, recorded by Jelly Roll Morton's Red Hot Peppers for RCA Victor in Chicago on 15 September 1926.

Trumpet	George Mitchell
Trombone	Edward 'Kid' Ory
Clarinet	Omer Simeon
Piano	Jelly Roll Morton
Banjo	Johnny St. Cyr
Double bass	John Lindsay
Drums	Andrew Hilaire

Morton's pieces had colourful titles, which his publishers could promote easily. *Black Bottom Stomp*, recorded in 1926, was a reworking of a composition written the previous year called *Queen of Spades*. The new title was designed to exploit the latest dance craze, the Black Bottom, which was replacing the Charleston in popularity, but it also refers to a run-down African-American area in Detroit that was famous for its vibrant musical life.

Morton demanded high standards from his players. The Red Hot Peppers was not a regular band but a group formed specifically for recording. He was able to recruit some of the best players of the day and rehearsals were sponsored by his publishers, allowing the music to be thoroughly prepared. *Black Bottom Stomp* lasts only three minutes, but Morton squeezes in a huge amount of detail, with solos for each of the main instruments.

Although Morton's players were well accustomed to improvising, his complex arrangement and demand for a high degree of ensemble at fast speeds meant that a large element of pre-composition was involved. The players were used to reading music from their work with other bands, but Morton was also prepared to give them very precise instructions when needed.

Structure

Black Bottom Stomp is based on two separate changes, which we have described as A (16 bars long) and B (20 bars long):

A

B
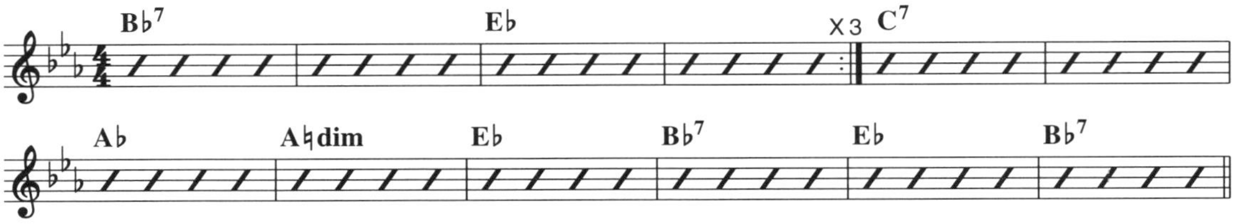

They are arranged as follows:

B♭ major	Introduction	8 bars	0'00"	Ensemble
	A1	16 bars	0'07"	Ensemble
	A2	16 bars	0'23"	Trumpet + ensemble
	A3	16 bars	0'38"	Clarinet solo
	Modulation	4 bars	0'52"	Ensemble
E♭ major	B1	20 bars	0'56"	Ensemble
	B2	20 bars	1'15"	Clarinet solo
	B3	20 bars	1'33"	Piano solo
	B4	20 bars	1'51"	Trumpet solo
	B5	20 bars	2'10"	Banjo solo
	B6	20 bars	2'28"	Ensemble
	B7	22 bars	2'48"	Ensemble

Rhythm section

The double bass and banjo play together throughout, except during the piano solo. Most choruses start with the bass playing a two-beat pattern in each bar, just like the 'oom-pah' accompaniment in ragtime which, in turn, came from the typical bass lines of military marches. However, the bass regularly breaks into a four-beat pattern, especially in the second half of a chorus, where the harmonic rhythm gets faster. These four-beat patterns have the character of a walking bass, a common feature of later jazz. One-beat and syncopated rhythms also add to the rhythmic momentum of the piece:

A1 Four bars of two notes, syncopation, then four notes per bar; the varied repeat starts with one note per bar
A2 Much variety: four notes per bar, two notes, syncopation and one note per bar
A3 Four bars of one note per bar, then more movement.

The bass line in the B sections is less varied, mostly using patterns of two or four notes per bar.

The banjo usually keeps time in crotchets or plays off-beat chords between the on-beat notes in the bass. The piano fills in the chords by comping, using similar rhythms to the banjo. The piano is recorded well back so it is difficult to hear.

Drums are fairly rudimentary and placed well back in the mix to avoid loud sounds distorting the recording. The bass drum, played with a hand-held stick, was large compared with those in modern drum kits. There is a suspended cymbal and, in B7, a snare drum.

On many early jazz recordings the drummer would keep time by playing a gentle clicking beat on a small woodblock or on the side of a drum. This practice continued into the early days of electrical recording.

Frontline

The trumpet plays the melody in most of the ensemble choruses. It is made up of short, two-bar phrases, with more elaboration in the second half of the chorus. George Mitchell's virtuoso trumpet solo in chorus B4 is more elaborate, but most of the ensemble choruses are similar and based on a narrow range of notes. Compare the trumpet line in choruses B1, B6 and B7.

Omer Simeon's clarinet exploits the wide range and ability of the instrument to play rapid and intricate passages. He uses an intense vibrato, common among jazz wind players of the time, and favours rapid descending arpeggios and ornamented figures. The clarinet countermelodies often lie above the trumpet melody, a common feature of early jazz in the New Orleans style.

The trombone part features long held notes, often connected by different types of glissando such as the **smear** (starting below the note and then sliding up to the correct pitch) and the **fall off** (sliding down from the correct pitch at the end of a note). These are features of the **tailgate** style of trombone playing (see *right*) of which Kid Ory was a pioneer. In faster passages notice how Kid Ory blends into the rest of the ensemble.

In the early days of jazz, bands would sometimes play on the back of a truck, placing the trombonist at the back (by the tailgate) to give adequate room for the use of the slide, especially when decorating notes with a glissando.

New Orleans polyphony

Although recorded in Chicago, *Black Bottom Stomp* reflects the traditional New Orleans style, especially in choruses B1, B6 and B7, which reflect the type of collective improvisation known as **New Orleans polyphony**. Morton and his players were masters of this style, and these are some of the best examples of it on record. One of the features of Morton's Chicago recordings is that he uses this style sparingly, reserving it for key points in the structure. The rhythmic drive and swing of these passages make them stand out. As a result, the B1 section helps to establish the B choruses as the main part of the piece, to which the A choruses act as dominant preparation, rather than as a long ending in the unexpected key of the subdominant (E♭ major).

The essence of New Orleans polyphony is the independence of the frontline parts: melody on the trumpet, counter-melody on the clarinet, and sustained notes and fills from the trombone, all heard simultaneously over the rhythm section's accompaniment.

Commentary

Introduction (ensemble)

The brief introduction uses tonic and dominant chords to establish the opening key of B♭ major. The trumpet and trombone slide up to long held notes, answered by a faster motif in the clarinet part:

Chorus A1 (ensemble)

The first A section initially seems to be a continuation of the introduction, but with greater harmonic variety. The first chord is G minor, and the use of G^7–Cm in bars 3–5 of the changes suggests a passing modulation to C minor, although tonic and dominant harmonies reappear in bars 6–8. The frontline play in the same rhythm, emphasising the syncopation in bar 5:

The eight-bar pattern is repeated with the bass beginning in semibreves instead of minims. Notice how the trumpet and clarinet play more elaborate melodic fills at the end of each eight-bar phrase.

Chorus A2 (trumpet and ensemble)

The opening four bars of the trumpet solo are answered by the whole ensemble playing the syncopated motif from the first chorus – an example of **antiphony**. The trumpet solo is slightly elaborated on its repeat and a clarinet fill leads into the next chorus.

Chorus A3 (clarinet solo)

Omer Simeon plays a rhythmic five-note figure that ascends through the clarinet's upper register to the highest note of the phrase:

This rhythmic figure is also played by the banjo, but the bass is heard only on the first beat of each bar to allow the rhythm to come across clearly. The clarinet solo continues in the answering phrase, with the syncopation present in the accompaniment.

Modulation (ensemble)

A descending chromatic phrase for the whole ensemble ends on B♭^{7}, in preparation for the new key of E♭ major.

Chorus B1 (ensemble)

This chorus features the collective improvisation typical of New Orleans polyphony. The clarinet covers a wide range, emphasising its high register and using highly decorated quavers and rapidly descending arpeggios. The trumpet melody is made up of short phrases, heard in **dialogue** with the clarinet.

The ensemble stops playing at bar 8 for a **break** (a short solo) for trumpet and trombone (notice the use of glissando). Jelly Roll Morton planned such changes in texture carefully to maximise their dramatic effect. Towards the end of the chorus the texture becomes busier: the bass plays a four-beat rhythm, a drum fill changes the usual percussion rhythm, and the momentum towards the next chorus is emphasised by repeated B♭s in the trumpet and the increased use of syncopation.

Chorus B2 (clarinet solo)

Omer Simeon now uses the rich, dark sound of the chalumeau register in contrast to the relatively piercing high register used previously. The solo starts with a repeated pattern of three quavers which cuts across the prevailing groups of four quavers:

This rhythmic device is called **secondary rag** and was a common technique in jazz improvisation of the day. It is a characteristic feature of ragtime (hence its name) and was often used in popular dances of the period such as the Charleston and Black Bottom. The accompaniment of short staccato chords separated by silences is known as **stop time** and allows the clarinettist to be heard clearly.

Chorus B3 (piano solo)

Jelly Roll Morton provides an example of his skills as a pianist in his use of **stride technique**, in which the left hand leaps between bass notes and chords on alternate beats:

Chorus B4 (trumpet solo)

The muted trumpet solo is in a high register and supported by another stop-time accompaniment. The ensemble here is not as precise as in most Jelly Roll Morton recordings: the syncopated chords are not quite together, and there are stray piano chords which are not in time with the rest of the band.

Chorus B5 (banjo solo)

The banjo solo starts with a chromatic secondary-rag figure, breaking into more standard strummed patterns in the second half of the chorus. There are no frontline instruments playing. The bass part stands out because the player uses **slap pizzicato** – a vigorous style of plucking that results in a percussive edge to the sound as the string rebounds against the fingerboard.

Choruses B6 and B7 (ensemble)

The whole band re-enters for two choruses in New Orleans style. The break is a syncopated figure on the cymbal, using a hand to choke the sound and in the busy final chorus the trombone at last has a chance to come to the fore, with the tailgate style of playing fully displayed in extravagant smears alongside long-held notes.

Both the trumpet and the clarinet are in their highest registers, with the trumpet playing variations on its solos in B4 and B6. The drum plays off-beats throughout the chorus and, by the end, the bass is playing a continuous walking pattern. The final phrase is repeated to make a 'tag' to complete the piece, ending abruptly on the fourth beat of the bar rather than on a strong beat.

Exercise 31

1. Explain the following four terms and give an example of each of them:
   (i) Collective improvisation (ii) Stop time
   (iii) A break (iv) Secondary rag.
2. Discuss the ways in which the technology available in the 1920s had an impact on the way in which early jazz was recorded.
3. How did ragtime influence Jelly Roll Morton's music?
4. Why is Jelly Roll Morton important in the development of jazz?

Count Basie: *Jumpin' at the Woodside*

This is one of the three jazz recordings set for exams in June 2009, January and June 2010, and January 2011.

If you are taking the exam in June 2011 or later, turn to the section starting on page 114.

William Basie (1904–1984) was a talented pianist and jazz arranger who joined the Kansas City Orchestra in 1929. It was at about this time that he became known as 'Count' Basie, following a tradition of early jazz musicians adopting the titles of aristocrats or royalty (Duke Ellington, King Oliver and Earl Hines among others).

Although Kansas City is a long way from Chicago and New York, the main centres of jazz and swing in the 1920s and 1930s, it had a busy nightlife centred on its bars and hotels. One of these was the Woodside Hotel, where many of the band stayed, and where *Jumpin' at the Woodside* was rehearsed.

After the leader of the Kansas City Orchestra died in 1935, Count Basie reformed the band and later moved it to New York, renaming it the Count Basie Orchestra. There he was able to take better advantage of the growing public demand for the new style of jazz known as swing, and to secure recording contracts that brought the band to the attention of an even wider public. Apart from a couple of short interruptions, the band continued until Basie's death in 1984, long after the era of big bands had ended and, in slightly different form, it is still performing and recording today.

Jumpin' at the Woodside, recorded 22 August 1938 in New York for Decca by Count Basie and His Orchestra.

Trumpets:	Buck Clayton Ed Lewis Harry 'Sweets' Edison
Trombones:	Dickie Wells Benny Morton Dan Minor
Alto sax:	Earle Warren
Tenor sax:	Herschel Evans (+ cl.) Lester Young
Baritone sax:	Jack Washington
Piano:	Count Basie
Guitar:	Freddie Green
Double bass:	Walter Page
Drums:	Jo Jones

An important element in swing was the use of a much larger band (a **big band** or **swing band**) than in early jazz, because the music often accompanied dancing in venues of considerable size. The recording of *Jumpin' at the Woodside* required 14 players and the list of personnel (*left*) shows how the frontline soloists of New Orleans jazz had expanded into **sections** of trumpets, trombones and reeds (saxophones, with Herschel Evans also playing clarinet).

Although solos were usually improvised, collective improvisation by the entire band was impractical with such large numbers, and so musical arrangements became essential in the swing era. These were often in the form of notated parts for the players, but *Jumpin' at the Woodside* is a **head arrangement** – so called because it was memorised (in the head) rather than written down. This was made easier by basing many of the ensemble sections on **riffs** – short, memorable patterns that can be adapted to different pitches to fit the current chord – played either in unison or in harmony.

Structure

The piece is made up of an introduction and five choruses. The first four are in 32-bar song form (four 8-bar sections in the pattern AABA). The fifth consists of six statements of the A section. The key is B♭ major throughout: there are no modulations but there is much chromatic decoration in the B sections:

Introduction	8 bars	0'00"	Rhythm section
Chorus 1 (AABA)	32 bars	0'08"	Ensemble. Reeds drop out for B (0'24"), where Earle Warren's alto sax solo is accompanied by detached brass chords (with a sustained chord to end)
Chorus 2 (AABA)	32 bars	0'39"	Ensemble. Brass drop out for B (0'55"), where Count Basie's piano solo is accompanied by the rhythm section (with the bass in a higher register)
Chorus 3 (AABA)	32 bars	1'09"	Trumpet solo (Buck Clayton) with ensemble backing. In section B (1'26") trombones drop out and saxophones accompany with sustained chords
Chorus 4 (AABA)	32 bars	1'40"	Tenor sax solo (Lester Young) with ensemble backing. Brass drop out for section B (1'58")
Chorus 5 (AAAAAA)	48 bars	2'14"	Duet for clarinet (Herschel Evans) and trombone (Dickie Wells) in the first A section, then clarinet solo with ensemble backing

Here is the basic harmonic outline of the A and B sections (there are various differences in detail in some choruses):

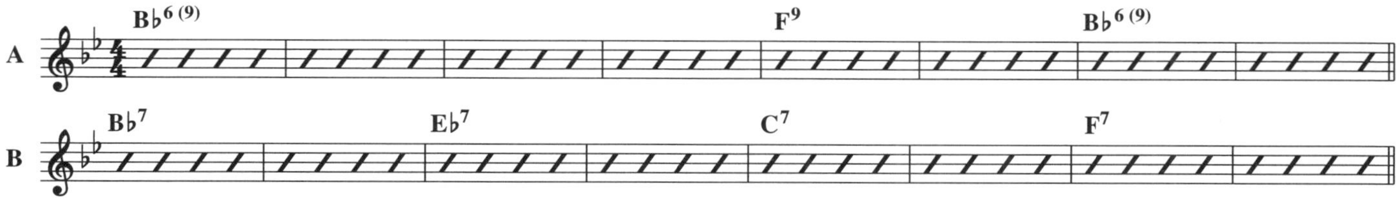

Notice the simplicity of the A section, which is based on just tonic and dominant chords (although both contain added notes).

The **bridge** (section B) is harmonically more interesting, using **secondary dominants** that give a suggestion of passing rapidly through related keys (B♭^{7} is the dominant seventh of E♭, and C^7 is the dominant seventh of F). It also has a slightly faster harmonic rhythm, with a new chord in every other bar. The contrast with section A is underlined by the changes of instrumentation in the B section (shown in the table *above*) each time it appears.

A secondary dominant is a chromatic chord that is the dominant of the *chord* (not the key) which follows it.

Rhythm section

The rhythm section of Basie's band was well known for its precise time keeping. The sound is well balanced, with the double bass and the drums playing lightly so as not to overwhelm the rest of the section. The piano and guitar are comping.

Walter Page's bass playing is recorded well back, so his four-beat walking bass style is difficult to hear clearly. Early jazz drummers used to keep time on the bass drum, but Jo Jones prefers to reserve the bass drum for unexpected accents. He uses a more modern method, characteristic of later jazz drummers, of time-keeping on the hi-hat or ride cymbals.

Exercise 32

Work out a group performance of the AABA pattern, using the chord charts on the previous page. Include a walking bass and use both diatonic and chromatic passing notes to keep the bass moving between chord notes. Compose a short riff that can be adapted to fit all of the chords required.

Frontline

The 14-piece band for *Jumpin' at the Woodside* is the most obvious difference between this piece and the early-jazz style of Morton's *Black Bottom Stomp*. The large number of players allowed Basie to create a full sound, but it also caused problems. Basie had been stung by criticism when he first arrived in New York that his band played out of tune. He replaced some of his players to secure the precise rhythms and intonation that he wanted for tutti chords.

The three sections of frontline instruments also allowed Basie to create a variety of textures – solo, ensemble in unison and ensemble in chords – which he combined in numerous different ways. Notice the following points about the accompaniment of solo sections:

- Instruments of the same type do not accompany a solo. The trumpets don't play during Buck Clayton's trumpet solo and the saxophones drop out for the solos from Earle Warren (alto sax) and Lester Young (tenor sax)
- The sound is balanced by bringing the soloist nearer to the microphone
- Accompanying instruments play quieter
- The texture is lightened by the style of the accompanying riffs – often staccato chords separated by rests
- Antiphony is used to add variety – as in Chorus 2, where the chordal brass riff from Chorus 1 is divided into antiphonal exchanges between trombones and trumpets, as shown *left*.

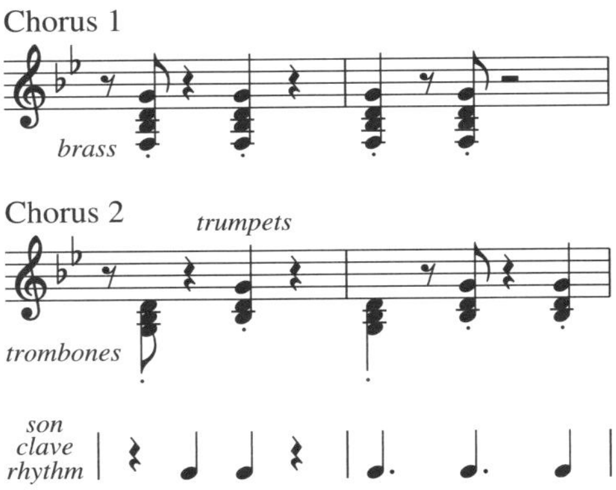

Commentary

Introduction (rhythm section)

Count Basie leads from the piano, setting the speed with left-hand crotchets in octaves. The rest of the rhythm section enters one by one, beginning with a swing rhythm on the hi-hat and drums, adding bass in a four-beat rhythm, and finally adding the guitar at the beginning of the first chorus. There is a diminuendo at the end of the introduction to prepare for the first chorus. The rhythm section keeps going until just before the entry of the trumpet solo at the end of Chorus 2.

Chorus 1 (ensemble with alto sax solo)

The three A sections of the 32-bar AABA structure are very similar. Saxophones play a four-note riff in unison, sustaining the last note while the brass answer with the syncopated chords shown in the first example *above left*. The rhythm of these chords is similar to the *son clave* rhythm that underlies much Latin-American dance music (the relationship becomes clearer in Chorus 2). Such Cuban influences were becoming increasingly common in 1930s' jazz.

Latin-American rhythms became very popular in jazz, often introduced by musicians from Cuba who worked in the USA, including in Kansas City.

In the B section, Earle Warren's alto sax solo starts with a slide up to the first held note. The accompanying brass chords are syncopated in an eight-beat pattern articulated as 3+3+2 beats.

Chorus 2 (ensemble with piano solo)

Count Basie, who was silent in the first chorus, begins his piano solo with a simple three-note riff high above the accompanying brass. It is heard three times in the first eight bars, followed by a concluding phrase. Although Basie was a capable virtuoso pianist, he was noted for his restrained, economical piano style and his effective use of rests. In the second eight bars he uses sequential repetitions of notes in the same range. The ensemble music from Chorus 1 continues with only subtle differences. The syncopated rhythms of the brass accompaniment are now split between muted trombones and answering trumpets.

In the B section, Basie plays a brief passage in stride piano style. As a young man he had received some guidance in piano playing from Fats Waller, a well-known master of stride piano. The melody remains economical, with phrases separated by rests, and ends with a passage in repeated 3rds in the right hand. The rest of the band is silent here, with only the rhythm section accompanying.

In the final A phrase, Basie takes a less prominent role, adding some off-beat chords to the texture. The ensemble stops abruptly for a trumpet break in the last two bars.

Chorus 3 (trumpet solo)

Buck Clayton's trumpet solo starts with a 'wah-wah' effect, usually achieved by using the **plunger mute**. Since the rest of the passage is muted, he may have found another way of covering and uncovering the bell of the instrument before pushing his mute in for the rest of the solo. He uses a fast vibrato, especially on longer notes. Notice the slide up to a top F immediately before the B section, followed by growling **scoops** (slides down and back up again) on the same note as the bridge begins.

The saxophones accompany with syncopated chords, each pair answered by a rising semitone from the trombones. The latter drop out for the B section, which is accompanied by sustained chords from the saxophones.

The last A section introduces a new riff which quotes the opening of Lester Young's piece *Lester Leaps In,* which Basie also recorded at this time. Since Lester Young is about to start his solo, the band would have enjoyed the joke.

Chorus 4 (tenor sax solo)

Lester Young actually enters in the last two bars of Chorus 3 with repeated quavers on B♭, for which he alternates rapidly between two different fingerings – listen for the changes in tone that result.

Chorus 4 proper then opens with a short motif which is given a decorated repeat before being extended into a longer phrase to complete the first A section. Not only does Young's soft-toned sax playing contrast in timbre with Clayton's trumpet solo, but also his style of improvisation differs. Where Clayton stayed close to the underlying changes, adding occasional blue notes and chromatic passing notes to largely triadic figures, Young concentrates on creating an interesting and more conjunct melodic line which often

results in **playing away from the chord** (as shown *left*) – a technique that was to become common in the bebop jazz style of the 1940s (see *opposite*). The accompanying brass chords set a new rhythm, featuring **fall offs**.

Lester Young starts his B section with repetitions of a six-quaver figure that create a **cross-rhythm** with the prevailing four-crotchet pulse, using a technique known as rhythmic displacement:

Chorus 5 (clarinet, trombone and ensemble)

The opening clarinet figure is adapted from the saxophone riff at the start of Chorus 1 and is answered in call-and-response style by the trombone. Herschel Evans' clarinet playing is bold and direct, supported by the typical fast vibrato of the day, while Dickie Wells answers with vocal-like growls, using a mute. After this exchange of ideas in the first A phrase the clarinet continues its solo, with riffs for the rest of the ensemble added in layers. There are six repetitions of the A section (and no B section) in this final chorus:

A1 Clarinet and trombone with rhythm section

A2 Clarinet solo continues, riffs are added for saxes (in unison) and trumpets (in block chords)

A3 A simple riff consisting of an upward glissando for unison trombones is added, trumpets move up an octave

A4 As Chorus A3, but with additional accents on drums

A5 Trumpets stop but trombone chords are added

A6 A diminuendo to the end.

Exercise 33

1. Why were the big bands popular in the 1930s?
2. Which features of Count Basie's band would New York audiences have regarded as new?
3. Explain what is meant by 32-bar song form and show how it is used in *Jumpin' at the Woodside*.
4. What is meant by each of the following?
   (i) a riff (ii) syncopation (iii) stride piano

Miles Davis: *So What* from *Kind of Blue*

This is one of the three jazz recordings set for exams in June 2009, January and June 2010, and January 2011.

If you are taking the exam in June 2011 or later, turn to the section starting on page 114.

Miles Davis (1926–1991) started learning the trumpet at the age of 13 and made such rapid progress that he was playing professionally within three years. After leaving school at 18 he entered the famous Juilliard School of Music in New York but left after only one term in order to work in the clubs with Charlie Parker (see page 119), whose quintet he joined at the age of 19.

The quintet was renowned for a type of jazz known as **bebop**, a fast-paced, dissonant style for a small group of players. Bebop was not particularly suitable for dancing. Bebop musicians regarded themselves as serious artists who composed and performed for discerning listeners. They took an interest in contemporary classical music, including composers such as Stravinsky and Prokofiev.

Further reading

Miles Davis: The Definitive Biography by Ian Carr. Harper Collins, 1982/1999, ISBN 978-0-006530-26-8. An absorbing account of Davis' life and music, including his later experiments with jazz-rock fusion.

Kind of Blue: The Making of the Miles Davis Masterpiece by Ashley Kahn. Granta Books, 2002, ISBN 978-1-862 075-41-2. An illustrated guide to the background of the recording of the album.

A score of *Kind of Blue*, including transcriptions of the solos in *So What*, is published by Hal Leonard.

Miles Davis left Parker's group in 1948 and began developing his own style of trumpet playing, which was quite different from what had gone on before:

- An understated, middle-register style with little vibrato
- Frequent use of pitch bends at the beginning and end of notes and a wide variety of tone
- An economy of style, tending not to use double time, and with more use of silence
- A flexible sense of timing which allowed him to anticipate or delay notes against the underlying pulse.

Davis' early recordings were on shellac disks, still limited to three minutes per side as they had been since the 1920s. However, by 1959 (when *Kind of Blue* was recorded) long-playing records had become established, allowing much more substantial works to be recorded as well as sets of shorter pieces grouped together by mood or some other linking idea.

Record companies promoted the new LP records with posed photographs of the artist(s) on the sleeve. Those of Miles Davis show him casually dressed but serious, sometimes wearing dark glasses, a long way from earlier images of jazz musicians as entertainers, or in formal suits playing in a swing band.

In the 1950s Miles Davis formed his own small groups – first a quintet and then a sextet – working with some of the greatest jazz musicians of the age. *Kind of Blue*, widely regarded as his greatest work, was recorded at a time when he had been exploring the possibilities of modal jazz, giving the players a mode to improvise on rather than the types of blues-based scales that had developed in the swing and bebop eras. He wanted his musicians to develop melodic ideas without relying on the chord changes to suggest conventional melodic formulas, and he encouraged them to use their own characteristic motifs rather than relying on stock ideas known as 'licks'.

So What, recorded 2 March 1959 in New York for Columbia Records by the Miles Davis Sextet and released on the album *Kind of Blue*.

Trumpet:	Miles Davis
Alto sax:	Julian 'Cannonball' Adderley
Tenor sax:	John Coltrane
Piano:	Bill Evans
Double bass:	Paul Chambers
Drums:	Jimmy Cobb

Structure

So What is based on the dorian mode, the simplest form of which you can find for yourself by playing a scale on a keyboard from D to the D an octave above, using only the white notes.

Dorian mode on D

Each chorus of the piece uses 32-bar song form (AABA), the type of structure that we have already seen in *Jumpin' at the Woodside*. However, instead of basing the A and B sections on different chord changes, Davis provides contrast by transposing the dorian mode up by a semitone, so that it starts on E♭, for his B section (see *right*).

Dorian mode on E♭

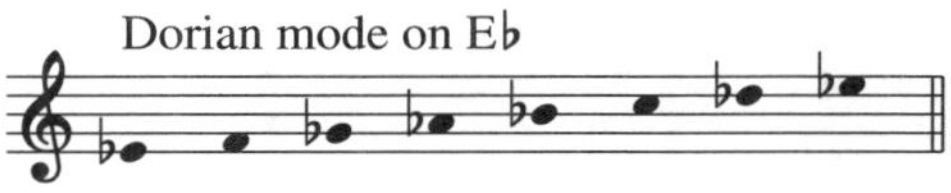

Another notable difference between *So What* and the earlier jazz works we have studied is the length of the piece, made possible by the greater recording time available on the LP records of the day. This allows extended solos for Davis, Coltrane and Adderley, each of which forms a double chorus (64 bars rather than 32):

Introduction	0'00"	11 bars	Piano and bass
Chorus 1	0'32"	32 bars	Theme (bass and ensemble)
Chorus 2 Chorus 3	1'29" 2'25"	64 bars	Trumpet solo (Miles Davis)
Chorus 4 Chorus 5	3'21" 4'16"	64 bars	Tenor sax solo (John Coltrane)
Chorus 6 Chorus 7	5'09" 6'03"	64 bars	Alto sax solo (Cannonball Adderley)
Chorus 8	6'59"	32 bars	Piano solo (Bill Evans)
Chorus 9	7'53"	32 bars	Theme (bass and ensemble)
Coda	8'50"	8+ bars	Fade-out ending

Rhythm section

Paul Chambers on double bass uses the typical walking bass style of the time, covering a wide range and using contrasting registers to create variety. The example from Chorus 2, printed on the next page, shows how quickly he can pass from one octave to another. The bass is the main time-keeping instrument, along with a regular swing rhythm on the ride cymbal.

Jimmy Cobb's drumming is light and understated, matching the mood of the piece. His style becomes more active as the work progresses, responding to the various soloists. In particular, he supports the bebop-influenced saxophone solos with more complex patterns, introducing unexpected syncopation and marking the start of each new section with some force before going back to the usual swing rhythm.

The piano part is also understated. The static nature of the harmonies means that Bill Evans has little to do in terms of making the changes clear. He prefers chords in the right hand, usually three or four notes, often dissonant, using combinations of 4ths or 2nds from the modal scale. His spacing of chords was influenced by the piano writing of composers such as Debussy and Ravel.

Commentary

Introduction

The introduction, for just piano and bass, was possibly written by Gil Evans, a well-known jazz composer and arranger with whom Miles Davis was working in the late 1950s (Evans produced an arrangement of it for a larger band, which he used a few weeks later in a television documentary on Miles Davis).

Although the introduction is not modal – it is an impressionistic sequence of unrelated major chords – it anticipates ideas in the theme that follows, including the upward leap of a 5th in the bass and the suggestion of the stepwise descending chords of the 'so what' motif (both shown in the next music example), as well as in the use of call-and-response between piano and bass. The flexible rhythmic style results from the use of rubato – there is no strict sense of tempo in the introduction.

Chorus 1 (theme) (ensemble)

The first chorus presents the theme – 32 bars in AABA form, in which the dorian mode of the A sections is transposed up by a semitone for the B section.

The double bass has the melody, a very unusual feature at the time, to which the piano responds with a motif whose rhythm seems to reply 'so what' (see *right*). This two-bar pattern is heard four times in all, with variations in the bass melody although the piano chords always remain the same. When this A phrase is repeated, trumpet and saxophones reinforce the first three pairs of piano chords, leaving the last pair for the pianist.

The bridge is essentially another repetition of the A section, but transposed up a semitone, and is followed by a restatement of the second A section.

Chorus 2 (trumpet solo)

Miles Davis begins his solo simply, with short phrases separated by silences, before embarking on a longer phrase in bars 4–7):

Davis widens the melodic range in section A2, which also has two short phrases followed by a longer one, but in a higher register. The B section provides greater contrast, not only because of the transposition of the mode, but also because Davis uses a yet wider range (covering two octaves) and more sustained phrasing. He also makes use of techniques such as **ghost notes** and **half-valving** in this section. With the reappearance of A, he returns to the restrained style of the opening, with silences separating short phrases.

> Ghost notes are not played fully so the tone is faint and hardly audible.
>
> Half valving involves pressing the keys half way down and modifying the tone with the embouchure (lip position). Davis uses the technique when sliding up to a note with a smear.

The use of short, mid-range motifs, played with little vibrato and often separated by long rests, was very different from the busy melodic style of bebop. However, Davis creates a conversational feel in his playing as well as adopting a well-tested approach to the overall shape of the melody by building to a climax two-thirds of the way through before relaxing again.

In the accompaniment, Bill Evans responds to the gaps in the melody by filling some of the silences with the chords of the 'so what' motif, often varied in rhythm. Like Davis, he uses a more sustained style in the B section, but the chord motif is still present in its transposed version.

Jimmy Cobb marks the first beat of the chorus with a splash on the crash cymbal and keeps time on the ride cymbal – notice how the cymbal rhythm momentarily disappears after the splash because he changes from brushes to sticks for this chorus, and makes greater use of the snare drum in its second half.

Chorus 3 (trumpet solo continued)

In his second chorus Davis makes greater use of held notes and falling 3rds, plus a wide range of effects, such as a forceful attack on the opening notes, a slight vibrato at the end of long notes, ghost notes and half-valving, and a variety of subtle slides and dips.

Davis focuses his melody on notes from the upper extensions to the chord of D minor (that is, on the 7th, 9th and 11th of the chord). Repeated open Ds (alternating with higher stopped notes) in the double bass create a tonic pedal effect for eight bars, after which Paul Chambers resumes his walking bass for section A2.

Bill Evans uses greater dissonance in his piano accompaniment, including 2nds, often moving chords up and down in parallel motion. The piano provides no bass: the chords are in the middle of the range, with some variety to match the mood of the music. Listen to the beginning of the chorus (at 2'25") where the chords are lower than before and the trumpet is in a higher register.

Chorus 4 (tenor saxophone solo)

John Coltrane initially takes his cue from the style of Davis' solo, starting with short modal phrases broken up by silences. He is backed by heavy accents on the drums. Similar motifs continue in A2, but in **double time**. Coltrane explores mirror-like arpeggiations of Dm^7, starting on a low D and working up to a high note before returning to D. Bill Evans increases the pace of his piano accompaniment to match the increased urgency of the solo.

In the B section Coltrane plays in the upper register, introducing more triplets and other rhythm patterns. The piano recedes into the background, to be replaced by busier use of the snare drum. The accents are irregularly placed, creating rich and constantly changing **polyrhythms** alongside the four-beat pulse of the ride cymbal and bass.

> Polyrhythm results from the use of distinctly different types of rhythm at the same time (such as triplet quavers and normal quavers). It was common in jazz throughout this period and by the 1950s jazz drummers had sufficient independence of hands (and feet) to play complex polyrhythmic patterns.

The A3 section has a contrasting dark tone and is in a low register. Every phrase begins with a motif of ascending semiquavers but each is extended and developed differently. Coltrane sometimes sharpens the seventh degree of the scale in ascending passages, as in a melodic minor scale, thus moving away from the modal feel that has been established.

Chorus 5 (tenor saxophone solo continued)

A1 is supported by a dominant pedal in the bass. The melody is a highly decorated version of a D-minor arpeggio, regularly going to a high D. The walking bass resumes in A2. Each phrase builds up by step, reaching a higher note each time. The highest notes of the solo are in the final A section (A3). The activity in the piano and drums builds up during the final semiquaver passages of this solo.

Choruses 6 and 7 (alto saxophone solo)

Cannonball Adderley's solo has more of a bebop style than the others. He is less influenced by the modal thinking of Miles Davis, and uses more chromaticism and dissonance.

Like Coltrane at the beginning of Chorus 4, Adderley starts with a feature of the previous solo before turning to his own style – in this case, the double-time semiquavers. He then introduces a variety of rhythms, including the crotchets and quavers that were the predominant note values used by Davis. In this way he deftly mixes elements of both the previous solos.

Adderley uses more vibrato than the previous two soloists and his use of contrast between virtuosic, intricate semiquavers and the tuneful slower passages lends a teasing quality to parts of his playing. Listen for the following features in Chorus 6:

A1 A rapid scale to the highest note, then a slower descent

A2 Like many of the choruses, this starts with more tuneful longer note values, followed by a faster display passage

B The soloist anticipates the change of chord by a whole bar. The piano puts the chord clearly in its expected position

A3 The slower motif appears at the end to form a link into the next chorus.

And listen for the following features in Chorus 7:

A1 The pianist makes a brief reference to the 'so what' motif. The short phrases with silences are similar to Miles Davis' solo

A2 The motif in the first bar is heard three times, with the bass playing a descending scale twice

B The upper notes are played staccato and the lowest allowed to sound their full length; piano chords change twice per bar

A3 The slower motif from the end of Chorus 6 reappears, slowing the music in preparation for the forthcoming piano solo.

Chorus 8 (piano solo)

Bill Evans has just one solo chorus. Its chordal style is unusual – most piano solos have a strong melodic line in the right hand, similar to a solo on any other instrument. He begins with short phrases of chords based on 4ths, answered by the trumpet and saxophones with a diminution (to two quavers) of the 'so what' motif. A2 is more melodic, with rising leaps of a 5th that recall the bass part in the theme.

The B section returns to a chordal texture, using dense, dissonant clusters of 2nds in the middle register of the piano, while in A3 the texture is reduced to parallel seconds, using a very restricted range of notes:

B
(last four bars)

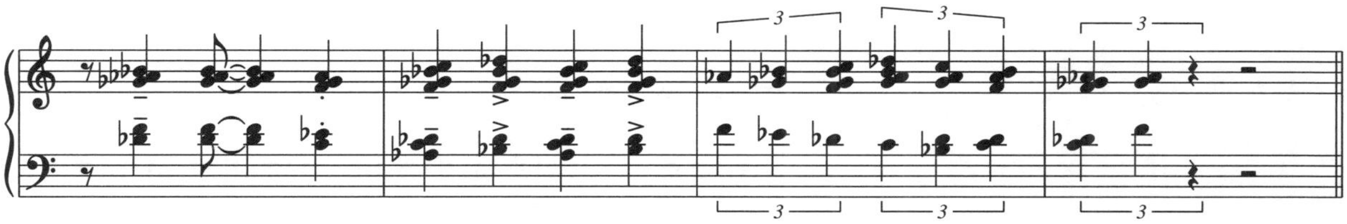

A3
(first four bars)

Chorus 9 (theme) (ensemble)

The theme is repeated at the end – a common practice in bebop. Paul Chambers on bass at first continues his walking bass, perhaps expecting that Bill Evans would play a second chorus like the other soloists. However, he picks up the bass melody at A2, where the frontline join in, as they did in the first chorus.

Coda (rhythm section)

Although a definitive conclusion was recorded, it was decided to release the track with a fade-out ending. This was a very new recording technique in the 1950s, but one that became extremely common in pop music over the next half century.

Exercise 34

1. How does the dorian mode on D differ from D minor?
2. The introduction to *So What* features rubato. What does this term mean?
3. Describe the ways in which Miles Davis produces a range of expressive effects from the trumpet.
4. How does the use of tonality in *So What* compare with the other works you have studied?
5. Listen carefully to the first and last choruses on the recording, and then explain how they differ.

Louis Armstrong: *Alligator Crawl*

This is one of the three jazz recordings set for exams in June 2011 and later. If you are sitting the exam before then, you do not have to study this work.

Turn to page 129 for notes about exam questions on the jazz recordings.

Louis Armstrong (1901–1971) grew up in New Orleans, the city closely associated with the early development of jazz. Despite a deprived and troubled childhood, his talent for the cornet led to employment in dance-hall and riverboat bands, playing alongside some of the greatest jazz musicians of the day. These included cornet player Joe 'King' Oliver, who became a lasting influence. Oliver moved to Chicago, where opportunities to make a living from jazz were greater, and invited Armstrong to join his band there in 1922. After two years Armstrong moved to New York, recording with Bessie Smith and other early blues singers, and playing in the prestigious Fletcher Henderson Orchestra.

Armstrong's abilities as a soloist became widely known through recordings and radio broadcasts, and his swinging rhythm and highly melodic style were much admired and imitated. Gradually all band leaders, not just those for whom Armstrong worked, began to leave space in their arrangements for longer solos, accompanied by a reduced band or just the rhythm section.

The Hot Five and the Hot Seven

Armstrong's wife Lil Hardin, herself a pianist and band leader, encouraged Armstrong to return to Chicago. She was keen to promote his career, and collaborated with him in composing and arranging pieces for The Hot Five, a small band set up for a series of commercial recordings with the Okeh company in 1925–1928 with Louis Armstrong as the leader.

Initially Lil Hardin played the piano, but by the end of the series Louis had left her. Some of the best players were recruited to take part in the recordings, including Kid Ory (trombone), Johnny St Cyr (banjo), Johnny Dodds (clarinet) and his brother Warren 'Baby' Dodds (drums). Like Armstrong, they were all born in New Orleans and had joined the exodus to Chicago to work with King Oliver.

The line-up changed a few times, and the Hot Five expanded and became the Hot Seven. Armstrong's solos were very popular – a collection of them was printed for other cornet and trumpet players to learn – and they played a larger role as the series of recordings went on. His playing influenced not just trumpeters but other soloists as well. It helped make the New Orleans style well known and provided the basis for the development of jazz in the 1930s.

There are a number of factors which account for Louis Armstrong's success. He was an outstanding improviser: his melodies were bold and dramatic, yet seemed to unfold completely naturally. He had a strong, rich tone, an enormous range, and virtuosic technique.

Louis Armstrong was also regarded as much more of a 'hot' player than most of his contemporaries – he swung the rhythm much more than those who tended to rely on the genteel type of syncopation used in ragtime – and he was much more flexible in his use of rubato, constantly delaying or anticipating beats. Armstrong was also an influential jazz singer, particularly in his innovative use of the voice to imitate instrumental solos, improvising vocally to nonsense syllables in the style known as 'scat' singing.

Structure

The outer sections of *Alligator Crawl* are based on four choruses of a 12-bar blues in F major. This was one of the most common sets of changes in jazz at the time. The precise chords used in a classic blues do vary, but almost all include the following features:

- Three phrases of four-bars
- Chord I at the start of the first phrase and chord IV at the start of the second phrase (B♭ in the key of F major)
- A slow harmonic pace (no more than one chord per bar – often the same chord will continue for two or even four bars).

Alligator Crawl, recorded 10 May 1927 in Chicago for Okeh Records by Louis Armstrong and His Hot Seven.

Trumpet:	Louis Armstrong
Trombone:	John Thomas
Clarinet:	Johnny Dodds
Piano:	Lil Hardin
Banjo/guitar:	Johnny St Cyr
Bass (tuba):	Pete Briggs
Drums:	Warren 'Baby' Dodds

The basic blues progression used by Armstrong is as follows, but in each chorus different chromatic and diminished harmonies are used to pass from one chord to the next:

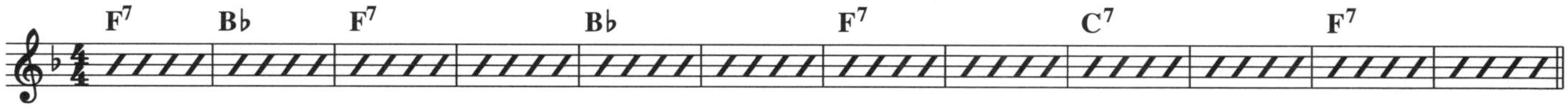

The middle section, an extended solo by Armstrong, is based on *Alligator Crawl* by the jazz pianist, Fats Waller. It is a **paraphrase improvisation**, in which the notes of the original are outlined clearly at the start. As the solo progresses Armstrong adds his own improvisational detail. Here is the structure of the entire track:

Fats Waller's own 1934 recording of *Alligator Crawl* can be heard at www.redhotjazz.com/Fats.html

F major	Introduction	2 bars	0'00"	Trumpet
	Chorus 1	12 bars	0'04"	Clarinet
	Chorus 2	12 bars	0'32"	Ensemble
	Link	4 bars	1'00"	
C major	Solo A B A¹	8 bars 8 bars 8+1 bars	1'09"	Trumpet
F major	Chorus 3	12 bars	2'07"	Guitar
	Chorus 4	12 bars	2'32"	Ensemble

Introduction (trumpet)

The brief unaccompanied introduction is played by Armstrong, beginning and ending on the dominant, C.

Chorus 1 (clarinet)

Although the 12-bar blues is based on primary triads (I, IV and V), these chords are not used in the type of functional, key-defining way found in the Baroque and Classical scores you have studied. This is largely the result of adding **blue notes** – particularly the flattened third and seventh degrees of the scale. Both are present in the opening bars, despite the F-major tonality – the blue 3rd (A♭) in the clarinet solo and the blue 7th (E♭) in the harmony – and Johnny Dodds makes prominent use of high E♭s in bars 7–8:

A smear is a slide up to a note from below, the fall off is a slide down at the end of a note, and a scoop is a slide down and back up again during the course of a note.

Notation cannot show every nuance of Dodds' highly expressive style, which includes glissandi, **smears**, **fall offs** and **scoops** to bend the pitch of many of the notes. He employs a fast, intense vibrato, that is typical of jazz clarinettists of the 1920s. The use of an arpeggio to move rapidly from high to low registers (the sextuplets in bar 10) is a very characteristic clarinet sound that we have encountered before, in the study of Mozart's Clarinet Concerto.

The piano and banjo keep time by **comping** in crotchets. The tuba plays the bass part, using a two-beat pattern with some faster rhythms to link the phrases. The trombone has low held notes. This style of accompaniment is used for most of the piece.

Chorus 2 (ensemble)

The second chorus features a style of **collective improvisation** known as **New Orleans polyphony**. Above a supportive chordal accompaniment and bass, each frontline instrument has its own melodic line and distinctive role:

- The trumpet has the melody, which here is in a high register and can be clearly heard above other parts in the recording.
- The clarinet has an elaborate countermelody, with rests at the beginning of phrases so that it answers the trumpet. Features of the clarinet solo from Chorus 1 reappear here: the melody from bar 3 is freely inverted and in bar 10 the clarinet has a held note followed by another rapidly descending arpeggio.
- The trombone has the tenor part in the texture, starting in minims and using glissandi and a pronounced vibrato.

Four bars link this section to the next, their purpose being to modulate to the dominant key of C major for Armstrong's solo in the central section of the work. They do this by emphasising the dominant (G^7) of the new key. A pedal G is sounded throughout the four bars, over which a diminished-7th chord resolves to G^7. The octave leaps on G in the trombone add to the effect.

Central section: trumpet solo (with rhythm section)

New Orleans jazz tended to favour collective improvisation and short solos. In contrast, Louis Armstrong's trumpet solo here is unusually long and reflects not only the growing importance of the soloist in jazz at this time but also his status as band leader.

The solo is in three eight-bar sections, forming an ABA^1 structure, the last bar of which overlaps with the first bar of a two-bar link. The A sections are in C major, with a modulation to the dominant (G major) by the end of the first four bars. The B section is in E minor for the first four bars, and G major for the second:

In the first A section the solo stays in quite a narrow range – only an octave for most of its eight bars. Ends of phrases are either cut short with a staccato note or rounded off with vibrato on the final note. Notice the varied approach to the four-note chromatic figure in bar 1, when it is repeated later:

- Bar 1: quavers, with a syncopation and a repeated E
- Bar 5: semiquaver–quaver rhythm, then twice in semiquavers with the accent displaced
- Bar 17 (where the A section returns): quavers in a higher octave, then twice in semiquavers, varied and split between octaves.

The B section, starting in the contrasting key of E minor, consists of short one-bar phrases. Armstrong ends the first four bars with a blues inflection on a held G, with vibrato added at the end of the note (**terminal vibrato**). The subsequent return to G major, with the trumpet moving to a higher register, builds up to a long high A immediately before the return of the A section.

In the varied repeat of the A section, Armstrong's playing is more obviously virtuosic and dramatic, covering a range of two octaves and including several wide leaps (a 10th and a major 7th in bar 17, and an 11th in bar 19). Even so, he still makes the phrases sound melodic and unfold naturally. For example, in bars 18^4–20^2 the phrase covers a 12th but comes to a rest on a mid-range G.

Armstrong extends A^1 to nine bars in order to create a short link into the final section. Notice how he approaches the top A in bar 24 with a **rip** (a rapid slide up through the harmonic series) and then ends on a repeated tonic C in bar 25. This note is also the dominant of F major, thus preparing for the return of the blues choruses in the home key.

Chorus 3 (guitar)

The contrast in texture between Johnny St Cyr's unaccompanied guitar solo and the band style of the rest of the piece disguises the return of the blues chorus at this point. He uses gently strummed chords decorated with some rhythmic movement, as well as both auxiliary notes and chromatic passing notes. The speed gradually gets faster as the solo progresses. Since no other instruments are playing, St Cyr is able to vary some of the harmonies in this chorus:

| F^7 | B♭ B♭m | F^7 C^7 | F^7 || B♭ | B♭m | F^7 C^7 | F F♯dim || C^7 | C^7 | F^7 B♭-B♭m | C^7 ||

Chorus 4 (ensemble)

The final chorus returns to the style of collective improvisation used in Chorus 2, but at a slightly faster tempo. There are more high notes this time, with a wide, wailing vibrato from both trumpet and clarinet. Note the interplay between the frontline instruments.

At times the clarinet and trumpet move together, for example in the swing rhythms at the end of the chorus. When the trumpet briefly breaks into **double time** for an elaborate fill at the end of a phrase, the clarinet follows a bar later. Elsewhere one instrument is rhythmically active while the other has long notes or rests. The trombone has long notes in its tenor range, with glissandi and vibrato less prominent than they were in Chorus 2.

The comping style of the piano continues, but the softer guitar chords do not cut through the texture as effectively as the banjo.

There is no coda: the piece ends with a stroke on a suspended cymbal, with the player using his hand to stop the note.

Further listening

Try to listen to other recordings by Louis Armstrong and the Hot Five, for example *West End Blues* or *Hotter Than That.*

Exercise 35

1. Which features of Louis Armstrong's playing help account for his fame as a jazz musician?
2. Name the American city from which many of the members of Louis Armstrong's Hot Five came, and explain the importance of that city in the history of jazz.
3. Why do you think that Armstrong chose to use a tuba for the bass part in *Alligator Crawl,* rather than the more usual double bass?
4. Towards the end of chorus 1, Johnny Dodds plays an arpeggio that descends into the lowest register of the clarinet. What is the technical term for that part of the clarinet's range?
5. Explain the meaning of each of the following terms:
   (i) comping (ii) smear (iii) rip (iv) collective improvisation.
6. Which two degrees of the scale are most likely to be altered when playing blue notes?

Charlie Parker: *Ko-Ko*

This is one of the three jazz recordings set for exams in June 2011 and later. If you are sitting the exam before then, you do not have to study this work.

Charlie Parker (1920–1955) was born in Kansas City in the USA. He taught himself the alto saxophone while at school, but initially didn't show any particular talent for the instrument. However, he practised intensely and modelled much of his playing on the style of Lester Young, who played in Count Basie's band in Kansas City (see page 104). Increasing skill and confidence led to work with various bands and then a move to New York in 1939, although it was not until 1940 that his playing started to attract attention and he was able to work as a full-time professional.

Parker was particularly interested in developing the chordal basis of his improvisation. Like Dizzy Gillespie and other musicians in New York he was interested in expanding the possibilities of jazz through exploring new scales or taking ideas from contemporary classical music. He practised arpeggios, exploring new ways of using added notes, and developed a facility to play a tune in any key required.

When Parker was improvising he astonished other musicians with the pace and resourcefulness of his playing. Like Louis Armstrong before him, his virtuosity set a new standard for soloists which young players were eager to listen to and copy. His fast, aggressive style of jazz was a striking contrast to the accessible melodic style of the big bands. It was known as **bebop**, rebop or simply bop.

Bebop

The big bands of the 1930s were starting to struggle in the early 1940s. The success of radio and records had made a serious impact on live performance and a series of retaliatory strikes by musicians simply cut them off from these new areas of employment. America's entry into World War II at the end of 1941 absorbed huge human and economic resources, and the war resulted in shortages of many materials, including shellac for making records.

As big bands got fewer in number, musicians turned to playing in smaller groups and bebop was the new style that emerged. It continued to feature traditional structures such as the 12-bar blues and 32-bar (AABA) song form, but its distinctive hallmarks were:

- Small groups of players
- Fast, virtuoso solos, chiefly on the trumpet or saxophone
- Rapid twists and turns in melodies that cover a wide range
- Extensive improvisation, with pre-arranged sections normally limited to the beginning and end
- Time kept by a walking bass and a regular beat or swing rhythm on the ride cymbal
- Irregular phrasing and unpredictable off-beat accents
- Dissonant interpretations of standard chord changes, exploring techniques such as flattened 5ths, chord substitutions, added notes, chromaticism and unusual scales.

The trumpeter Dizzy Gillespie and the pianist Thelonious Monk were the first to pioneer the new style in 1940, trying it out in small groups after hours. A year later they were joined by Charlie Parker. To some extent the fast, intense style of bebop appears to be a reaction against the big band style, but its chief musicians were also successful performers in big bands. Dizzy Gillespie continued to work with big bands throughout his career.

Audiences, then and now, found it difficult to grasp the dissonance and irregular phrasing of bebop, which seemed to contradict the regular song structures outlined by the rhythm section. It had a much more intellectual appeal than music of the swing era – it was music to listen to, appreciate and discuss, rather than music to accompany singing and dancing.

Bop musicians tended to regard their work as separate from the commercial mainstream of white-dominated swing bands. The fact that bebop exalted improvisation above arrangement reinforced a developing African-American identity. Gillespie and Monk adopted a consciously intellectual appearance, including berets and goatee beards, and bebop-influenced music soon started to appear in the concert hall, particularly in the works of Leonard Bernstein.

Strikes in the American music industry in 1942–1943 mean that the early development of bebop went virtually unrecorded. *Ko-Ko* was therefore among the first examples of bebop to be recorded.

The chord changes from the song *Cherokee*, written in 1938 by the British band-leader Ray Noble, had long appealed to Charlie Parker and soon became a jazz standard used by many musicians. The melody (not used by Parker) is very simple, but it is supported by richly chromatic harmony, with many added 7ths, 9ths, 13ths and other added notes, that form the basis of the changes.

The song has an AABA structure – usually described as **32-bar song form**, although notated by Noble in 64 bars rather than 32. The most distinctive feature of *Cherokee* is its bridge (the B section) which, instead of starting in the expected key of F major, opens with a chord of F♯^{13} and then wends its way back to F (and then on to B♭ as the A section returns) by means of a **circle of 5ths** (see page 135). Here is a slightly simplified outline of the changes in the original song:

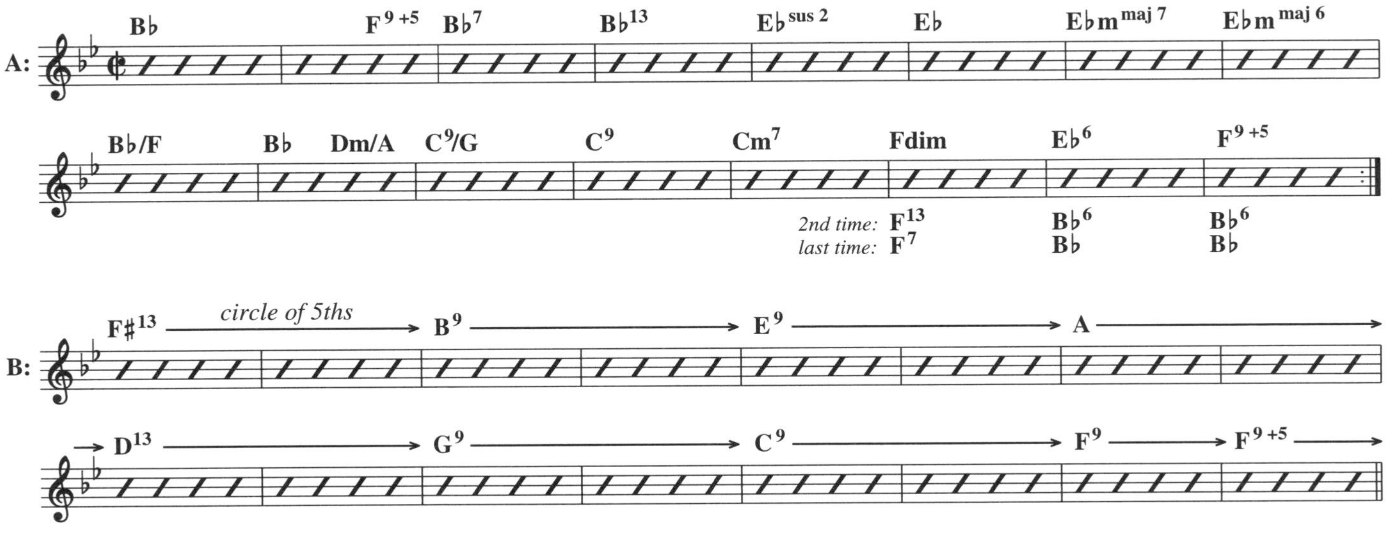

Structure

Ko-Ko starts with a 16-bar introduction, which is followed by two choruses of solo improvisation from Charlie Parker (based on the *Cherokee* changes). A drum break then leads to the return of the introduction (without its last few bars) to form a coda:

Introduction	32 bars	0'00" 0'06" 0'12" 0'19"	Bars 1–8 Bars 9–16 Bars 17–24 Bars 25–32	Alto saxophone and trumpet in octaves Trumpet Alto saxophone Alto saxophone and trumpet in 3rds
Chorus 1 (AABA)	64 bars	0'25" 0'38" 0'51" 1'03"	Bars 1–16 A Bars 17–32 A Bars 33–48 B Bars 49–64 A	Alto saxophone solo
Chorus 2 (AABA)	64 bars	1'16" 1'29" 1'42" 1'56"	Bars 1–16 A Bars 17–32 A Bars 33–48 B Bars 49–64 A	Alto saxophone solo
Drum solo	27 bars	2'07"		
Coda	28 bars	2'30" 2'36" 2'43" 2'49"	Bars 1–8 Bars 9–16 Bars 17–24 Bars 25–28	Alto saxophone and trumpet in octaves Trumpet Alto saxophone Alto saxophone and trumpet in 3rds

Rhythm section

Curly Russell is silent in the introduction, which is accompanied only by drums. During the choruses he plays a fast **walking bass** in crotchets, often using pairs of notes of the same pitch. In a style characteristic of bebop he makes frequent use of non-chord notes or added notes such as 9ths and 11ths, and often totally avoids the root notes of the harmony. Listen for passages in which he plays in the high register of the double bass.

Ko-Ko, recorded 26 November 1945 in New York for Savoy Records by Charlie Parker's Reboppers.

Alto saxophone:	Charlie Parker
Trumpet/piano:	Dizzy Gillespie
Bass:	Curly Russell
Drums:	Max Roach

Max Roach was one of the first to develop a new technique of drumming which went beyond its traditional time-keeping role. Although he uses the ride cymbal to articulate the crotchets of the walking bass, he uses the rest of the drum kit to develop some of the rhythmic ideas which he hears in the solos. He responds with unexpected bass drum or snare drum accents (sometimes known as 'bombs') on offbeats. The drumming is subtle, but it increases in activity to match the shape and intensity of the solo music.

A similar process is heard in the piano, played by Dizzy Gillespie. He accompanies Charlie Parker's solo with isolated chords, either staccato or sustained, to highlight changes in harmony – compare this with Lil Hardin's repeated chords which keep time in *Alligator Crawl*. Some chords are placed on strong beats, but more often he places mid- or high-register chords on weak beats. The left hand is used very little. The result is a light texture in the rhythm section.

Chords tend to be more dissonant than the lush original harmonies of *Cherokee* – for example, changing major intervals to minor or diminished ones. Gillespie also uses **chord substitutions**, meaning the replacement of a chord with a (usually more colourful) one that

Some mystery surrounds the piano part in *Ko-Ko*. Dizzy Gillespie had not expected to play trumpet in the work since Miles Davis was booked for the part. However, Davis left before *Ko-Ko* was recorded and so Gillespie played trumpet in the outer sections as well as piano in the choruses.

However, music had to be recorded in complete takes in those days, not in separate sections, and while the drum break gave Gillespie time to switch instrument for the ending, there is no similar gap after the introduction. It is therefore thought likely that a session pianist helped out in the first few bars of Charlie Parker's improvisation.

can serve a similar harmonic function. A favourite substitution was to replace a dominant chord with one that is a tritone away, as in the example *left*, where F^7 in bar 1 is replaced by B^9 at the same position in bar 2.

Commentary

Introduction

The introduction consists of four phrases of eight bars each and was probably written by Gillespie. He and Parker had a close working relationship, including practising each other's solos. This helped them to play fast, intricate bebop melodies accurately in unison or octaves – they choose octaves for the first eight bars.

Gillespie's trumpet solo in the next eight bars is in continuous quavers, but Parker follows this with an alto saxophone solo that divides his eight bars into three distinct phrases, a glimpse of the solo to come. Finally, both come together in 3rds for the final eight bars of the introduction.

The only accompaniment is from the drums, whose off-beat accents match those in the melody. The cymbal, double bass and piano are held back until the first chorus and the start of the changes.

Chorus 1 (Alto saxophone solo)

The first chorus is mostly diatonic, with occasional chromatic notes that mirror the changes in the chords, or as auxiliary or passing notes. The big-band jazz of the 1930s added 9ths, 11ths and 13ths to chords to enrich the harmony, but Parker was much more interested in using such added notes as important ingredients in his melody – the effect was to make his improvisations sound more dissonant than those of earlier jazz musicians.

If you listen carefully (the transcription printed *opposite* will help you follow it) you will notice that the solo is made up of different motifs – some are used more than once, often in varied form, and some can also be found in other recordings by Charlie Parker. He had a stock of hundreds of phrases and motifs which could be adapted at speed when improvising. The technique of weaving melodic formulae such as these into a continuous melodic line has been described as **formulaic improvisation**. In the hands of lesser players such a method could sound predictable, but Parker uses it to produce musical results and gives his solo a natural sense of shape and development.

At the beginning, most of the phrases match the four-bar phrasing of *Cherokee*. Compare bars 17–20 with bars 1–4 and you will see that the first two A sections start with similar three-bar phrases, each followed by a bar's rest.

In the B section, the melody of bars 33–34 is repeated a tone lower in bars 37–38, but there are also examples of asymmetric phrasing. For instance, the phrase beginning in bar 47 continues into the first two bars of the final A section. Parker follows this with a four-bar phrase (bars 51–54) and then a six-bar phrase (bars 55–60).

Notice also how Charlie Parker often places accents on weak beats. The drums and piano contribute their own unexpected accents in response to his playing as well as filling in strong beats when the solo starts on an offbeat.

In the last four bars the quavers stop and a sustained dominant (F), echoed by the piano an octave lower, signals the end of the chorus. The drummer adds a syncopated rhythm on the bass drum in response (until now the bass drum has only been used for single accents or pairs of notes). Compare the way the band marks the end of this chorus and prepares for the next to the similar methods used by Louis Armstrong at the end of choruses in *Alligator Crawl.*

Chorus 2 (saxophone solo)

Charlie Parker begins his second chorus with a two-bar quotation from a well-known and challenging clarinet solo, *High Society*, a jazz display piece made famous by the New Orleans clarinettist Alphonse Picou. Here are the main features of this chorus:

		Solo	Accompaniment
A	1'16"	Quotation from *High Society* Mixed phrase lengths: 4+3+5+4 bars Moves rapidly across a two-octave range	Pizzicato walking bass, starting in high register Descending chromatic countermelody in piano
A	1'29"	Asymmetric phrasing continues: 2+6 bars	Piano chords are more regular
B	1'42"	Descending arpeggio figures 4+2 quavers create cross-rhythms Rapid descending scales in semiquavers	Modulations using circle of 5ths More active drum part
A	1'56"	Opening similar to A1 and A2 in Chorus 1	Bass in a higher register

Drum solo Drum solos were unusual in early jazz and so the inclusion of one here is an indication that drummers were beginning to shake off their image of being simply time-keepers. The solo is faster than the rest of the piece and the drums are tuned higher than was usual, providing a brighter, more attacking tone for this solo.

Max Roach begins with clearly defined rhythmic patterns; by the end he is rapidly switching between the various parts of the drum kit while maintaining a constant rhythmic pattern. Listen to the variety in his playing, with its use of syncopation, figures that cut across the regular pulse and a range of timbres created by using both the centre and edge of the drum heads.

Coda This final section is essentially a repeat of the introduction, without its last four bars, although notice the addition of cymbals. Parker's solo uses the same continuous quaver rhythm as Gillespie but whereas Gillespie's improvisation is scalic, Parker uses patterns of decorated, downwardly-spiralling arpeggios.

Exercise 36

1. Which features of *Ko-Ko* would you choose to show what is meant by bebop?
2. Make a table of the main features of Chorus 1, similar to the table printed above for Chorus 2. Then list the similarities and differences between the two choruses.
3. Explain what is meant by a chord substitution.
4. Compare the sounds and textures heard in *Ko-Ko* with those heard in *Alligator Crawl.*
5. What is the relevance of Ray Noble's song *Cherokee* to Charlie Parker's *Ko-Ko*?

Gil Evans / Miles Davis: *It Ain't Necessarily So*

This is one of the three jazz recordings set for exams in June 2011 and later. If you are sitting the exam before then, you do not have to study this work.

For more on Miles Davis, see page 108.

Miles Davis (1926–1991) was one of the most influential jazz musicians in the second half of the 20th-century. He made rapid progress on the trumpet at school and at the age of 18 left for New York, where he was soon working with his musical idols, Charlie Parker and Dizzy Gillespie. He played most of the trumpet parts in Parker's recording sessions although, as mentioned earlier, Gillespie took over his role in *Ko-Ko*. Davis' own trumpet style was more economical than Gillespie's, less obviously bebop influenced. He preferred a middle-range sound, with a controlled use of vibrato, and a sensitive use of phrasing and silences.

In 1948, at the age of 22, Miles Davis formed his own band of nine players, working closely with the self-taught Canadian arranger, Gil Evans, who had arranged pieces for the Claude Thornhill band in New York. Thornhill's band was central in the development of a new style of **cool jazz**, employing instruments not previously used in jazz (such as the orchestral horn and tuba) to create striking new textures. Members of the band were encouraged to play without vibrato and the style was precise and considered, with a strong element of pre-composition in the arrangements – all of which greatly influenced Davis' own work.

In 1957 Miles Davis signed a recording contract with Columbia, who were keen to promote new styles of jazz. The result was three albums with Gil Evans as arranger, the second of which was *Porgy and Bess*. It consists of arrangements of 13 numbers from George Gershwin's popular opera *Porgy and Bess*, first staged in 1935. In the opera, *It Ain't Necessarily So* is sung by a cynical drug dealer named Sporting Life. The sinuously twisting main theme forms the basis of Evans' interpretation, and he retains the tempo and key of the original. However, he doesn't include the faster contrasting sections that occur in Gershwin's opera, although he does refer to their rising chromatic harmonies in his bridge sections (B1, B2 and B3 *below*).

Structure

A nine-bar introduction is followed by four choruses in 32-bar song form, the last of which has an AAAA phrase structure rather than the usual AABA:

B minor	Introduction	9 bars	0'00"	
G minor	Chorus 1	32 bars	0'35"	A1
			0'49"	A2
			1'03"	B1
			1'17"	A3
	Chorus 2	32 bars	1'31"	A4
			1'45"	A5
			1'59"	B2
			2'14"	A6
	Chorus 3	32 bars	2'28"	A7
			2'42"	A8
			2'55"	B3
			3'10"	A9
	Chorus 4	32 bars	3'24"	A10
			3'38"	A11
			3'53"	A12
			4'07"	A13

This table looks complicated because each eight-bar phrase has been labelled for reference later. It will be easier to remember the basic structure if you remember that it is similar to the repetitions of standard 32-bar song form used in *Ko-Ko* (but see *right*).

The 32-bar song form is interpreted very flexibly. For example, A7 at the start of Chorus 3 is a continuation of A6. The main melody returns in A9 and then continues into A10 at the start of the next chorus.

It Ain't Necessarily So from *Porgy and Bess* (by George Gershwin), recorded 29 July 1958 for Columbia Records in New York by Miles Davis and the Gil Evans Orchestra.

Five trumpets (soloist: Miles Davis)
Four trombones
Three orchestral horns
Tuba

Alto saxophone (Cannonball Adderley)
Flute / alto flute / clarinet (2 players)
Alto flute / bass clarinet (1 player)

Double bass (Paul Chambers)
Drums (Jimmy Cobb)

The band

The 19-piece band used for the recording was unusually large for jazz in the 1950s. It included Cannonball Adderley, Paul Chambers and Jimmy Cobb, who were to record the album *Kind of Blue* with Davis the following year (see page 108).

The presence of only one saxophone in the line-up is surprising. Most big bands of the swing era in the 1930s had a large sax section. In contrast, Evans' band is dominated by the brass – 12 players in addition to the solo trumpet. The softer tone of the three horns – instruments more usually found in the symphony orchestra – is used to help blend the sound of the trumpets and trombones (similar to the way in which horns were often used to blend the different sounds of the woodwind section in a Classical orchestra). The tuba provides depth to the large brass section – the double bass would not be strong enough to provide this function by itself.

Some other orchestral instruments appear in the reed section, in which three of the four players are required to swap instruments for different pieces on the album. There are two alto flutes and a bass clarinet available for darker woodwind sounds in low registers where they do not cut across the solo line.

The rhythm section

The large orchestral sound means that a chord-playing instrument is not needed – rather in the way that a harpsichord was no longer necessary after orchestras increased in size during the Classical period.

A riff is a short, repetitive pattern that can be adapted to different pitches to fit the current chord.

In a rimshot the drum head and the rim of the drum are hit simultaneously with the same stick, producing a strongly-accented note.

The double bass and drums provide the backing for the long solo, supported by chordal **riffs** from horns and trombones. Chambers uses the four-beat walking bass style which was by now firmly established in jazz.

There is a steady swing rhythm on the ride cymbal and a **rimshot** on the fourth beat of most bars. Cobb uses some variety of tone and rhythm, but there is less sense of a musical commentary on the solo compared with Max Roach's drumming in *Ko-Ko,* where the small group encouraged more activity in the drum part.

Harmony

See page 109 for more on the dorian mode and on Miles Davis' interest in modal jazz.

The harmonies in the A sections are based on a chord of Gm^7 and use notes from the dorian mode on G, shown *left*. The original harmonies of the song also have a strongly modal feel – Gershwin alternated chords of G minor and C major in the main part of the accompaniment, although he also incorporated some chromatic harmonies. Davis had a strong interest in using modal scales in place of chord changes. He believed that set chord progressions limited the melodic possibilities of improvisation because players were more likely to depend on stock phrases they had used before. The musicians could be more inventive with their melodies if there were relatively few chord changes.

The B sections are more exciting in both texture and harmony, providing a clear contrast to the solo passages.

Commentary

Introduction

The slow introduction contains a brief reference to another song from *Porgy and Bess – I Got Plenty of Nothin'* – which didn't receive an arrangement of its own on the album. This opening section is in the key of B minor, unrelated to the modal G minor of the rest of the track, and has a carefully calculated instrumentation:

- Trumpet melody in a high register
- Low tremolo on D and F♯ in woodwind
- Trombone minims, descending chromatically
- Pizzicato triplets in double bass, forming a six-bar decorated tonic pedal
- Drums played with brushes.

In the last three bars, the solo melody ascends in step over chords of Bm^7 and Am^7. At the climax of the phrase a chromatic chord (D–F–A♭–C) substitutes for a dominant 7th in order to modulate to G minor for the rest of the piece.

Chorus 1 (A1 and A2)

The tempo for the main part of the track is twice the speed of the introduction. The drummer has changed to using sticks and the theme is introduced in **paraphrase** style, meaning that it outlines features of the original melody. Davis uses short motifs separated by silences, focusing on the descending perfect and diminished 5ths that are such a feature of the tune. Having only hinted at the melody in A1, Davis comes closer to quoting it in the first two phrases of A2:

Notice the use of **ghost notes** (marked with crossed noteheads) where the tone is almost inaudible. The horns play syncopated staccato triads in a riff of four chords (shown *right*) which forms the basis of the accompaniment for the rest of the piece. The accent on the last quaver of the bar, instead of the first, reinforces the swing feel of the music.

(B1)

The band has a fuller part in all three B sections. Davis plays a descending scale, starting on the highest note heard in the introduction, and the accompaniment begins to ascend chromatically, with rich chords in brass and woodwind, and a steady crescendo throughout.

After four bars, as the solo trumpet drops out, the other trumpets add their brightness to the texture. The chords are in close harmony, the whole section moving in one rhythm. Notice how Gil Evans writes unexpected accents on weak beats to create syncopation. The crash cymbal is used to strengthen some of these accents and is also used at the end of the chorus.

(A3) The solo phrases are longer and more sustained in A3, with fewer silences. A new accompaniment motif in the trombones appears at the end of the chorus. The held chord (shown *left*) is underpinned by G in the bass so the A in the uppermost part forms a major 9th above the basic chord of Gm^7, adding a richness to the harmony that is enhanced by the use of a type of vibrato produced by rapidly moving the trombone slide in and out.

Chorus 2 (A4 and A5) The motif printed above is repeated at the end of A4, but now with the held chord replaced by a syncopated rhythm. In A5, instead of exploring a restricted number of mid-range notes, Davis plays a three-note figure in a long descending sequence, followed by an ascending scale. The whole passage takes the melody from the highest range to the lowest and back again. The accompanying horn riff is changed rhythmically and then freely inverted towards the end of A5.

(B2) The chords are played in legato minims. A short chord, backed up by bass drum, creates a dramatic break in the middle of the ascending scale. As the chords continue to ascend, notice the bass moving in alternate descending 5ths and ascending 4ths. The complex harmonies build up to a final dissonant chord, taking full advantage of the number of instruments in the orchestra to create a very rich spacing of the chord.

(A6) Davis begins with the falling augmented 4th from bar 5 of A1. The texture has been reduced to trumpet and rhythm section plus quiet brass riffs. Miles Davis uses scale passages and references to the intervals of the melody. He regularly returns to G, D and D♭, for example at the beginning and end of phrases. The motifs in the brass accompaniment are fragmented, altered in shape and rhythmically displaced (shifted to start on unexpected beats). There is a feeling of uncertainty and exploration.

Chorus 3 (A7 and A8) The style of A6 continues into A7 at the start of this third chorus. In A8, the accompanying riff is used as expected in the first half, and then inverted in the second half. The diminuendo by the band reduces the accompaniment to pianissimo.

(B3) The dramatic return of the full band, playing in a triplet rhythm, shows Evans' skill as an arranger: chords in different sections of the band move in contrary motion with each other and then, after a four-beat silence, move together in the same direction. In the second half of this bridge, the soloist's ascending scale from B2 returns, along with the accompaniment in ascending minims. The latter is now scored for horns and trombones only, so that Miles Davis will not be hidden by the band trumpets – they simply enter for a single **stab chord** of G minor, with a high G as the top note.

(A9) The original melody returns, with the accompaniment of A1.

Chorus 4 (A10, A11, A12 and A13) In A10 Evans continues the sense of recapitulation by continuing with the original melody and now the accompaniment of A2. In A11 the horn riffs are varied, but soon revert to the original two bars just before A12. Remember that there is no bridge in this final chorus – the B section is replaced by another appearance of the A section, which we have called A12. The texture is thinner, with no heavy brass, the horns play quietly, and the dynamic reduces to pianissimo in the rhythm section at the end of A13. The soloist starts a final descending scale on a high D. This final section is based around a repeated A, which sounds unfinished, although the double bass has a final tonic G to end.

Further reading

Miles Davis: The Definitive Biography by Ian Carr. Harper Collins, 1982/1999, ISBN 978-0-006530-26-8. An absorbing account of Davis' life and music, including his later experiments with jazz-rock fusion.

Exercise 37

1. How does the trumpet style of Miles Davis differ from that of Dizzie Gillespie?
2. What impact did developments in studio technology have on the recording of *It Ain't Necessarily So*?
3. Explain the different roles played by George Gershwin, Gil Evans and Miles Davis in the creation of this version of *It Ain't Necessarily So*.
4. Explain each of the following terms:
   (i) riff (ii) rimshot (iii) ghost note (iv) bridge.

Questions on the jazz recordings

In Section B of the listening paper you will hear an extract from one of the three jazz recordings you have studied. You will be expected to be able to recognise which part of the complete recording it comes from and to answer a short series of questions worth 15 marks. These might ask you about:

- Who the performers are
- The performing techniques that they are using (such as the use of a harmon mute or glissandi)
- When and where the recording was made.

Or you may be asked:

- To describe the music of a particular passage (such as the accompaniment or the use of a motif)
- To compare the chorus or a solo improvisation with one from elsewhere in the whole recording.

In Section C of the paper, which we look at in more detail in the next chapter, you might be asked:

- To compare the jazz styles used in two of the recordings you have studied
- To compare the role of an instrument in one of the three jazz recordings with the way a composer scored it in one of the three orchestral scores.

Section C questions

For Section C of the paper you will have to write an essay – the only long piece of writing that you are asked to do for AS Music. You should take care over how you structure and express your answer because your quality of language will also be assessed.

You will have to answer **one** question from a choice of three. The questions will give you the opportunity to focus more closely on one or two of the six pieces you will have studied, but don't bank on your favourites coming up – you will have to be ready to write about any of them. Some questions might ask for a comparison between two of the pieces, perhaps about techniques of handling instruments, others might explore your knowledge of the context of one of them (explained *below*), or you may be asked about issues to do with reception, transmission or performance practice.

The better you know the music, the more convincing your answer is likely to be. Each time you make a general remark, such as how an instrument is used, you will make more of an impression on the examiner if you refer to *precise examples* from the piece concerned.

Your essay must answer the question set – irrelevant material, even if correct, is unlikely to receive credit. For example, if the question asks about Schubert's writing for strings, you will only waste time if you start by outlining the composer's life and works, or if you discuss other matters, such as form or tonality. Try to answer concisely and remember that you won't get marks for repeating points you have already made.

Context

You will be expected to have developed a 'contextual awareness', that is an understanding of the broad background to the orchestral scores and jazz recordings that you have been studying; and your knowledge of any specific details that are known about the genesis of each piece – in other words, how it came into being. You need to know when and where the music was composed or first heard, and what sort of occasion it was for. For some pieces, little detail may be known, in which case you may have to focus on what concerts or recordings were usually like at the time.

Try to form a rough picture in your mind of places, types of building (venue) and audiences. What sort of people were they? Why had they come and what did they expect? Who were the musicians? How did they earn a living?

After closely studying the six pieces you should know quite a lot about the instruments and the ensembles involved. Compare the sort of orchestra used in Mozart's Clarinet Concerto with the band that recorded *Jumpin' at the Woodside*. How similar or different are the instruments and the ways in which they are combined? How has technology changed the sound that they make? How do the performing techniques differ?

Essay-writing

The practice questions *below* will give you a good idea of the sort of essay you will be asked to write in the exam. Jot down half-a-dozen points about each of them as they occur to you and then practise your essay-writing technique by developing your notes into full answers for at least two of them. Remember that the way you express yourself and present your ideas will be assessed, so it is important to aim to be coherent and clear in the way you use words and shape sentences. Be careful about spelling: if you misspell the names of musicians or titles of pieces it will give a bad impression to the examiner.

Although there is a lot to do in the time, don't rush to spill everything you know about a particular piece down on the paper: take a few moments to think carefully about what the question is asking: what does the question expect you to do? Is it to compare, to describe, or to explain? Which pieces? How many of them? Which aspects? Make sure that what you write is really relevant: don't go into details of how clarinets are constructed if the question is about improvising techniques.

Above all, the examiner wants to know how well you really know the music. The most convincing way to show this is by referring to an example – a melody, a riff, a chord, a rimshot – to illustrate the point in your answer. Be as precise as you can: explain exactly *where* in the music your example occurs, for instance 'the first trumpet riff can be heard at the start of the second chorus'.

Practice questions

1. In Bach's Orchestral Suite No. 3 and Mozart's Clarinet Concerto what were the principal differences in the ways that the orchestras were made up and how the two composers wrote for them?
2. Compare the trumpet parts in Bach's Orchestral Suite No. 3 with the sort of sound and techniques of playing produced by Miles Davis.
3. Compare the way music was made available to audiences in 1920–1960 with what often happened in the 18th and early 19th centuries. Refer to the background to at least one of the orchestral scores **and** at least one of the jazz recordings you have studied in your answer.
4. Discuss the use of imitation in the orchestral and jazz repertoire you have studied. Refer to examples from at least one orchestral and one jazz piece.
5. If you were asked to prepare a performance of an 18th-century orchestral piece what aspects would you need to think about? Would you consider it important to respect the composer's intentions?
6. Compare the contributions to the pieces you have studied of **either** Jelly Roll Morton *and* Count Basie **or** Louis Armstrong *and* Charlie Parker.
7. Discuss the role of the soloist in jazz. What would be expected of them? In what ways did the role change over time? Refer to examples from at least **two** of the jazz recordings you have studied.
8. Describe the effect of advances in recording technology in the 1950s on the work of Miles Davis and explain how his situation compared with the experiences of earlier musicians. Refer to examples from at least **two** jazz pieces you have studied.

Further reading

You will probably have some favourites among the works you have been studying and might like to find out more about them. Or you may be asking some questions of your own – how was an early clarinet made? How were early microphones different from those in use today? How did jazz spread beyond America? How is vibrato produced on a violin?

Depending on what you want to know, you may find the resources listed below helpful. The ultimate reference work for musicians is *The New Grove Dictionary of Music and Musicians* edited by Stanley Sadie and John Tyrrell (Oxford University Press, 2004, ISBN 978-0-195170-67-9). There is a separate *New Grove Dictionary of Jazz* by Barry Kernfeld (Oxford University Press, 2003, ISBN 978-1-561 592-84-5). Most major libraries have a reference copy and some allow borrowers to access the online version free of charge. However, it is extremely detailed and you may find that it tells you so much that it is difficult to get all the information straight in your head. *The Cambridge Music Guide* edited by Stanley Sadie and Alison Latham (Cambridge University Press, 1990, ISBN 978-0-521399-42-5) is a useful and more manageable resource.

Internet sites

There is a wealth of information available on the internet, but remember that standards of accuracy and reliability vary. If you are a regular user of Wikipedia you will already know that while it is often a good starting point for research, the information there is not always correct in every detail. Some record companies put the sleeve notes from CDs on their websites and these can be a useful source of additional information.

Do remember that many music websites focus on biographical information about musicians, which will often not be relevant to your course. Try to use the web to answer questions about the music itself. Focus on the areas of study and building up your technical knowledge about the music you are studying.

The BBC Radio 3 website has useful information on both classical music and jazz. You can also listen to recent broadcasts online and follow links to other useful sites.

Recordings

It is advisable to study more than one recording of each of the set orchestral scores. For the set jazz repertoire it is essential to study the precise recordings listed on page 59. Don't forget that radio and TV are free sources of music: search the listings weekly, including channels that you don't normally turn to.

Reference section

Major and minor triads

In major keys, the chords on the tonic, subdominant and dominant are described as **major triads** because they all include the interval of a *major* 3rd above the root, while the chords on the supertonic, mediant and submediant are described as **minor triads** because they all include the interval of a *minor* 3rd above the root.

Notice that minor chords occur in major keys. Similarly, major chords occur in minor keys.

Both major and minor triads contain an interval of a perfect 5th between the root and 5th of the chord. But the triad on the leading note is different – it has a diminished 5th between its outer notes and is therefore known as a **diminished triad**.

Keys

To see how keys are related study the diagram *right*. Keys next to each other in the circle are closely related. Going clockwise, each key is the dominant of the previous one (D is the dominant of G). Going anticlockwise, each key is the subdominant of the previous one (C is the subdominant of G). Step inside the circle to find relative minor keys. For example, the three most closely related keys to G major are D major, C major and E minor (each shares all but one of its notes with G major).

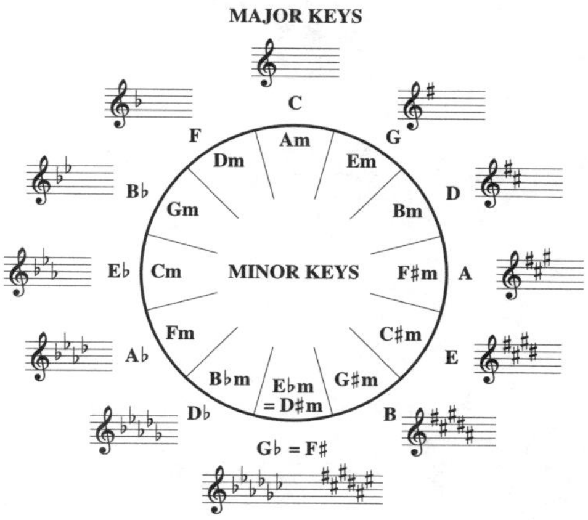

Cadences

There are four main types of cadence, illustrated *below* in a variety of keys, of which the first two are the most common:

- A **perfect cadence** consists of the progression V–I and has a conclusive effect, rather like a full stop.
- An **imperfect cadence** ends on chord V and has an inconclusive effect, rather like a comma. There are various choices for the first chord, including I, ii, iib and IV.
- A **plagal cadence** consists of the progression IV–I and has a conclusive effect, although less so than the perfect cadence. It is sometimes likened to the sound of a sung 'amen'.
- An **interrupted cadence** consists of chord V followed by any chord *except* I (V–vi is a possible choice). It sounds rather as if a perfect cadence has been interrupted by a momentary change in the harmonic direction and is sometimes used before the final perfect cadence, which then states the tonic key more clearly.

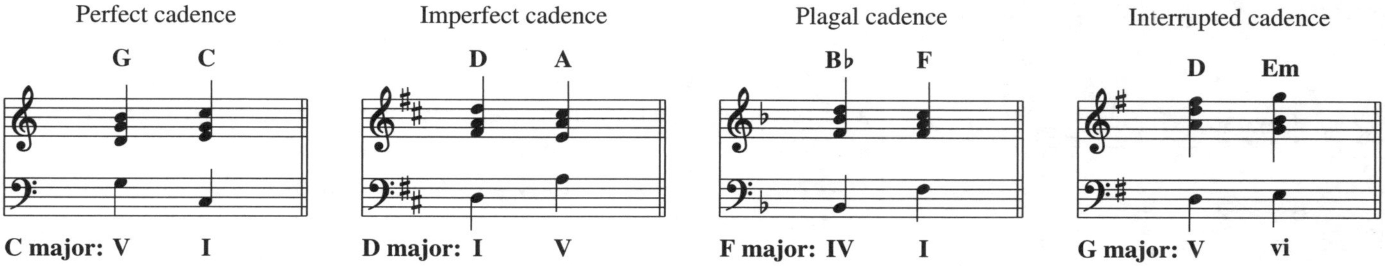

Inessential notes

We discussed passing notes on page 25. Here are some other types of inessential note. Learning their names is less important than seeing how stepwise movement is involved in approaching and/ or quitting the dissonances they create:

Appoggiatura:

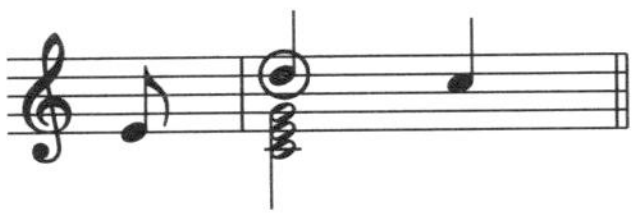

Auxiliaries:

Anticipation:

Échappée:

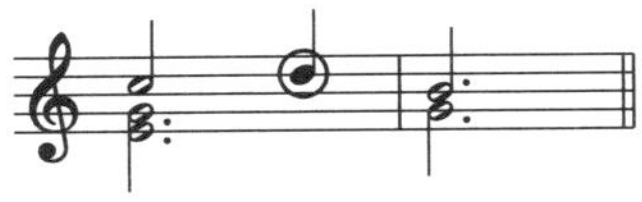

Suspension:

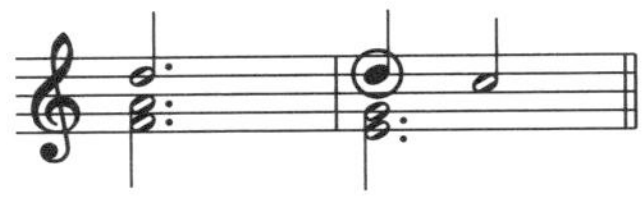

- The **appoggiatura** is similar to the accented passing note, except that it is approached by a leap rather than by a step.
- **Auxiliary notes** decorate harmony notes by moving to the note above (an upper auxiliary) or below (a lower auxiliary) and then back again.
- Notes of **anticipation** move by step to one of the notes of the *next* chord while the current chord is still sounding.
- The **note échappée** (escape note) is like a passing note, except that it leaps a 3rd, in the opposite direction, to the next harmony note instead of moving by step.
- A **suspension** occurs when a harmony note from a previous chord hangs on to sound as an expressive dissonance above a new chord. This dissonance is 'resolved' when the note concerned moves by step to a note of the new chord.

Part writing

(a) ✘ (overlap) ✔ (no overlap)

G: Ic V (7) I Ic V (7) I

(b)

F: iib Ic V (7) I

(c)

(d)

Here are some basic rules of good practice for part writing, especially when writing exercises for four voices:

- Avoid large leaps in the alto and tenor lines.
- Do not allow the parts to overlap as you move from one chord to another. For instance, the soprano should not leap below the alto note of the previous chord, as shown *left* in example (a).
- Remember that the leading note has a natural pull upwards towards the tonic. In chord V, the third of the chord is the leading note of the scale and so should rise to the tonic in that part.
- When using chord V^7, not only should the leading note rise to the tonic, but whichever part has the 7th should fall by step to a note of the next chord, as shown *left* in example (b).

A word about parallel intervals

In traditional harmony, each part should be independent. This means that you need to avoid parts moving in parallel unisons, octaves or perfect 5ths, as shown *left* in example (c), because these types of movement do not sound truly independent of each other. Of course, if parts don't actually move, but simply repeat their previous notes, as in example (d), that is fine.

We are referring only to traditional part-writing here. Consecutive parallel octaves are frequently used in piano and orchestral music, and parallel root-position triads (which generate consecutive 5ths) are common in modern pop music. However, for your examination portfolio, you need to show an understanding of the way that inner parts connect from one beat to the next, whether the harmony is moving in block chords or in a more linear, melodic style.

Even if your full-texture exercises are written for piano or guitar, you should always avoid consecutive 5ths or consecutive octaves between the melody and the bass.

The circle of 5ths and other chord progression

If the roots of a chord progression keep moving down in perfect 5ths, or up in perfect 4ths, they will pass through all 12 notes of the chromatic scale, eventually returning to the starting pitch and producing a pattern known as a **complete circle of 5ths** (to simplify the notation, we have changed from sharps to flats at C♯, which is the same pitch as D♭):

Notes which sound the same but are written differently, such as C♯ and D♭, are called **enharmonic** equivalents.

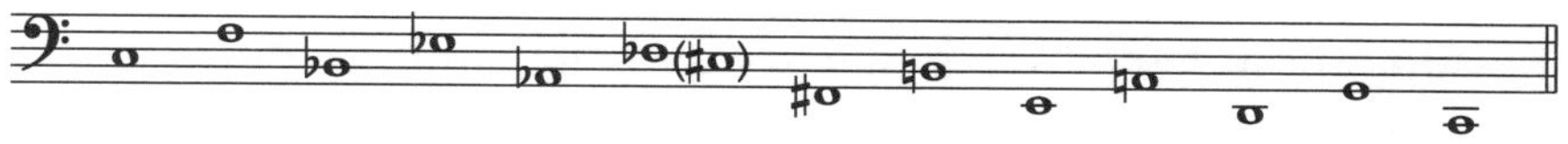

Complete circles of 5ths are hardly ever used because they involve so many notes outside the key that the sense of tonality is weakened. In practice, composers prefer an abbreviated version known as a **diatonic circle of 5ths** in which a falling diminished 5th (or rising augmented 4th) is used between the subdominant and the leading note. This has the effect of keeping all of the notes within the current key and provides a shorter route back to the tonic:

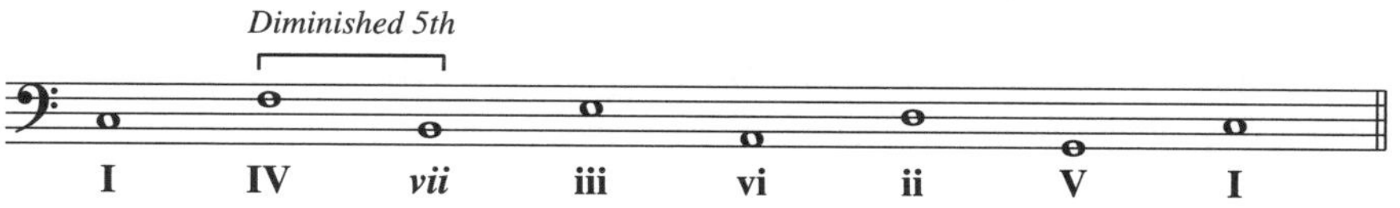

Falling 5ths are not the only type of progression that works well – chords whose roots fall in 3rds also sound good, and are often combined with falling 5ths, as in the following chord patterns:

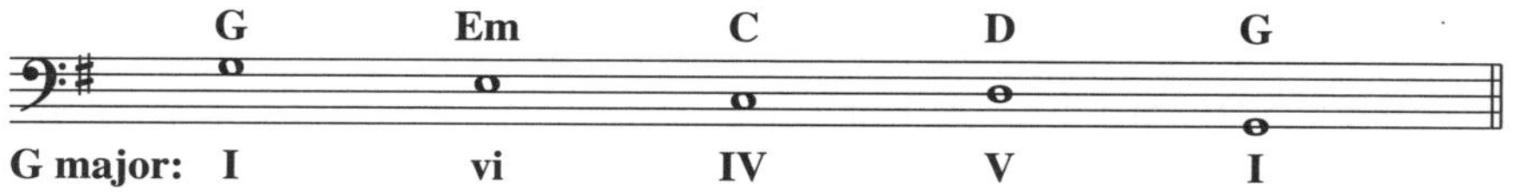

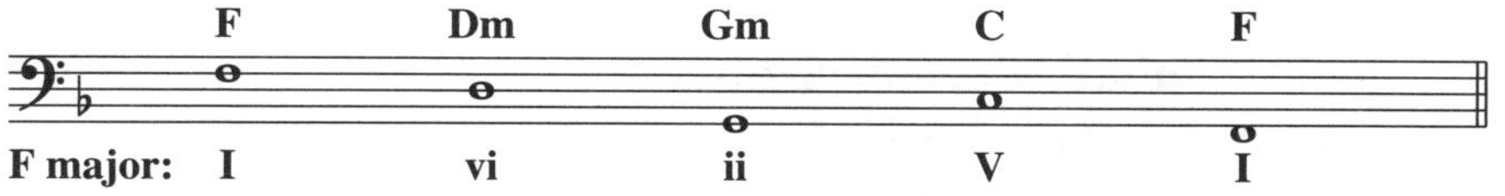

The clarinet in B♭ and other transposing instruments

The most common type of clarinet is the clarinet in B♭, which is a transposing instrument. 'In B♭' means that B♭ sounds when C is played. It follows from this that every note on the B♭ clarinet sounds a tone lower than written. To put it the other way round, if your music is in D major, it will have to be written out a tone higher, in E major, for the B♭ clarinet. This is something to bear in mind when combining the clarinet with other instruments. For example, music in D major, which is an easy key for the violin, has to be written in E major for the clarinet – a tricky key for less-accomplished players.

Other transposing instruments work in a similar way. For example, a horn in F sounds F when C is written – all of its notes sound a perfect 5th lower than written. And, as we learned in our study of the Mozart and Schubert scores, the clarinet in A sounds an A when C is written – all its notes sound a minor 3rd lower than written.

Textures

Throughout the AS course, techniques for combining instruments will keep coming under the spotlight and you should expect one or two questions about this aspect of the music. If you are asked to describe a texture, give as much detail as you can, explaining such points as which instrument has the melody (including any doubling involved), which has the bass line and how the accompaniment is distributed. You could be asked to give a term that describes the texture at a specific point, in which case the following list should prove helpful:

- **Monophonic** (an unaccompanied melody)
- **Homophonic** (one main melody with accompaniment)
- **Polyphonic** or **contrapuntal** (several melodic parts heard at the same time)
- **Heterophonic** (different versions of the same melody heard simultaneously, such as a simple version of the melody in crotchets and a decorated version in semiquavers)
- **Antiphonal** (an alternation of contrasting performing resources, such as between a soloist and a brass section).

These basic labels can often be amplified with more detail. For example:

- If the texture is monophonic, are all the instruments playing in **unison** (that is, at the same pitch) or are some doubling at one or more octaves above and/or below? If so, which?
- If the texture is homophonic, is the accompaniment in the same rhythm as the tune (producing a **chordal** texture of the sort often heard in hymn singing) or does the accompaniment have a life of its own (often described as **melody and accompaniment**)?
- If the texture is contrapuntal, is it in two, three or four parts? And is it **imitative counterpoint** (each part sharing in the same melodic material)? If so, can you be specific about where each instrument begins, which comes in next, and what the pitch interval is between each imitative part? On the other hand, is the texture one of **free counterpoint**, in which there is no imitation but in which several quite different melodies are combined?

Textures often change within even a short extract and are sometimes combined. For instance, within a basically homophonic passage, a main melody might be accompanied by a **countermelody** to add contrapuntal interest.